Social Security Reform

The Lindahl Lectures

Social Security Reform

Peter A. Diamond

OXFORD
UNIVERSITY PRESS

OXFORD

UNIVERSITY PRESS

Great Clarendon Street, Oxford OX2 6DP

Oxford University Press is a department of the University of Oxford.
It furthers the University's objective of excellence in research, scholarship,
and education by publishing worldwide in

Oxford New York

Auckland Bangkok Buenos Aires Cape Town Chennai
Dar es Salaam Delhi Hong Kong Istanbul Karachi Kolkata
Kuala Lumpur Madrid Melbourne Mexico City Mumbai Nairobi
São Paulo Shanghai Singapore Taipei Tokyo Toronto

with an associated company in Berlin

Oxford is a registered trade mark of Oxford University Press
in the UK and in certain other countries

Published in the United States
by Oxford University Press Inc., New York

British Library Cataloguing in Publication Data
Data available

Library of Congress Cataloging in Publication Data
Data available

ISBN 0–19–924789–7

10 9 8 7 6 5 4 3 2 1

Typeset by Newgen Imaging Systems (P) Ltd., Chennai, India
Printed in Great Britain
on acid-free paper by
Biddles Ltd., Guildford and King's Lynn

Series Foreword

The Lindahl Lectures on Monetary and Fiscal Policy have been instituted by Uppsala University with support from Nordbanken as a biannual event to honour the memory of Erik Lindahl (1891–1960). Lindahl was a great economist who held a chair in economics at the University between 1942 and 1958. A concise but thorough account of Lindahl's scientific contributions with a selective bibliography has been published by Otto Steiger.[1] A more extensive account, including many valuable biographical details, has been presented by Jan Petersson.[2]

Lindahl's contributions fall mainly within four areas:

1. National income accounting.
2. Public finance.
3. Monetary and macroeconomic theory.
4. Stabilization policy.

National accounts are essential for the design of tax policy and stabilization policies. Lindahl developed a consistent intertemporal framework for the basic concept of income by relating it to capital, the pricing of capital goods, and capital gains and losses. He also devoted much time and effort to initiating the empirical measurement of national income movements over time in Sweden. His extremely meticulous work with social accounting concepts has proved to be of such lasting value that it led Sir John Hicks to call him 'the father of Social Accounting theory'.[3]

In public finance Lindahl greatly advanced Knut Wicksell's benefit approach to taxation. His theoretical model for distributing the costs of public goods through a political analogue to markets for private goods is a standard reference in tax policy. He also did a substantial amount of empirical work, directed towards measuring

---

[1] 'Erik Robert Lindahl', in John Eatwell, Murray Milgate, and Peter Newman (eds.), *The New Palgrave*, New York, Stockton Press, 1987, Vol. 3: 194–8.

[2] 'Erik Lindahl', in Ragnar Bentzel *et al.* 'Economics at Uppsala University. The Department and its Professors since 1741', *Acta Universitatis Upsaliensis. Studia Oeconomica Upsaliensia*, 23(1993): 71–92.

[3] John R. Hicks, 'Recollections and Documents,' *Economica*, 40(157): 2–11.

the total tax burden and analyzing the effects of double taxation of saving through company taxation. He participated in an international comparison of the burden of taxation in different countries.

Best remembered and most highly regarded among Lindahl's contributions is his pioneering work in macroeconomics as a leader of the Stockholm School. In fact, the term 'macroeconomics' was first introduced into economic parlance by Lindahl. If Wicksell was the first to formulate the idea of 'disequilibrium dynamics', Lindahl was one of the first, and perhaps the first, to develop this into a general area of research. He devised a novel methodology for economic dynamics and introduced many concepts that have become standard in economics, such as temporary equilibrium and the 'natural rate' of unemployment.

Like all Swedish economists of his time, Lindahl was intensely interested and involved in current economic problems and policies. He directed much of his work at finding solutions to the pressing problems of the interwar years, namely, the stabilization of prices, output, and employment. To the Swedish public, he became best known for his fight against inflation after World War II, as an adviser to the *Riksbank*. According to Lindahl, a stable price level should be the declared aim of an independent Central Bank. This target should be reached by using the bank's control of the term structure of interest rates to influence the market's anticipations of future prices.

As Lindahl realized, monetary policy by itself is not sufficient to deal with unemployment problems during depressions. He proposed to complement monetary policy by compensatory fiscal policy, letting the budget balance vary inversely with the business cycle. As Ragnar Frisch stated in 1947, 'Lindahl . . . was one of the first, if not the first, to bring out the view that the essence of problems of public finance resides in the relations that link public finance to monetary policy, and to emphasize the role of the combined monetary and fiscal policy as tools of promoting full employment on a high level of real income and economic welfare.'

This describes perfectly why Uppsala University has thought it fitting on commemorate the work of Erik Lindahl by a series of lectures on monetary and fiscal policy.

                                                    Bengt-Christer Ysander

Uppsala,
March 1991

Preface and Acknowledgements

Sometimes you get lucky. At a time, about 30 years ago, when I was spinning my wheels trying to decide what to work on next, Bill Hsiao invited me to join a panel for Congress reviewing the financial status of Social Security.[1] The experience made me eager to join a successor panel that considered alternatives for reform for the overindexed system the US had legislated in 1972.[2] On and off, I have continued to work on US Social Security ever since, with both academic research and participation in public debate.

As the former communist countries were trying to adapt their economies, like many economists, I was fascinated and jealous of the economists who were involved in advising for the transition. I approached Jeff Sachs to see if I could be a part of the activity. He arranged for me to go to Warsaw to study Polish social security. Another lucky stroke. While Poland had very real issues of poverty among the elderly and a budget that was short on resources, the intellectually interesting issues for an outsider unfamiliar with Polish politics were the proposals for long-run reform, particularly the proposal to imitate the Chilean reform. I wrote about Poland and Chile (1994). This led to an invitation from Barry Bosworth, Rudi Dornbusch and Raul Laban to write the chapter on social security for a Brookings conference about Chile that they were organizing. I wrote this, together with Salvador Valdés-Prieto (1993), from whom I learned a great deal. As interest grew worldwide in the Chilean experience, I had a valuable piece of human capital.

The opportunity and the honor to give the lectures upon which this book is based, on October 21–23, 1999, (along with the roughly simultaneous invitation to give the Angelo Costa Lecture in Rome (Diamond, 1999b)) drew me into issues in western Europe. This was another lucky stroke that exposed me to the very interesting

[1] Panel on Social Security Financing consulting to U.S. Senate Finance Committee, 1974–75.
[2] Consultant Panel on Social Security of the Congressional Research Service, 1975–76.

reforms (and nonreforms) happening in Sweden and elsewhere in Europe. This led to further invitations to study Germany (forthcoming), Spain (2001*b*) and the Netherlands (2001*a*).

My goal for the first (public) lecture of the series was to illustrate my general approach to social security by analyzing some of the issues most relevant for then current discussion in Sweden. My goal for the following two lectures was to give an overall view of some of the research findings and research needs about social security. The lectures were organized by considering the labor and capital markets separately. In completing this book, I have stayed fairly close to the lectures as delivered. I have added a brief introduction, as a guide to the material.

I am grateful to Annika Sundén for a great deal of information and suggestions in preparing these lectures, to Ed Palmer for discussions and to Saku Aura, Tom Davidoff, Joanna Lahey and Marek Pycia for research assistance. I also benefited from the comments of a reviewer arranged by Oxford University Press. The research reported on here was supported by the National Science Foundation, under grant: SBR-9618698. The views expressed are my own.

I am grateful to Bertil Holmlund and his colleagues in Uppsala for showing Kate and me such a good time during our visit. The lectures were a pleasure as well as an honor.

Contents

For Kate, with love and gratitude

Introduction

Social security is a great topic to think about. Consideration of its effects on the economy leads one to think about much of economic analysis. Thinking about how to make its effects better leads to even more.

It is obvious that social security is important for retirement decisions. For many workers social security implies greater resources on reaching the age of eligibility for benefits than they would have had otherwise. For some other workers, social security means waiting until eligibility for benefits before retirement can be afforded. Retirement incentives are also affected by the details of the rules determining benefits. Since benefits are paid as an annuity, the perceived payoff to continued work depends on life expectancy. And it depends on the extent to which workers appreciate the insurance benefits inherent in annuities. And it depends on the relationship between the size of benefits and the age at which they start.

Social security also matters for the labor supply of younger workers. Their take-home pay is reduced by payroll taxes. The effect of social security on their labor supply also depends on how they perceive and appreciate the way that current earnings increase the retirement benefits that they may eventually receive.

Social security also affects the level of savings workers undertake to provide for their retirements. And its impact on government finances can affect the government's contribution to national savings. Beyond its impact on labor and capital supplies, social security plays an important role in the allocation of risks in the economy. By holding assets, a partially or fully funded social security system spreads the risk in returns to capital over a wider population. By having a system that is not fully funded, social security spreads the risks to cohort-wide wages over more generations than current workers.

Contemplation of the effects of social security on the labor and capital markets involves study of multiple links and subtle interactions. This makes for very interesting analyses. The story becomes even richer when considering a normative evaluation of the effects of social security on economic equilibrium. For a variety of reasons, including missing markets, time-inconsistent behavior, and asymmetric information, normative analysis of social security must be approached as part of second-best theory, not as an application of the Fundamental Welfare Theorem. And second-best theory, while more difficult, is far more interesting to use than invoking that theorem.

Consideration of policy recommendations for social security must go beyond normative economic analysis to also consider politics. Because of its high visibility, legislative consideration of social security lends itself to thinking about the links among policy recommendations and political and economic outcomes. This happens when considering the difficulty in passing any single piece of legislation. It is even more interesting when considering the links among a legislated structure, future economic and demographic circumstances, and future legislation. Indeed, when I headed a panel that considered issues in the privatization of social security in the US (Diamond, 1999*a*), the disagreements among members of the panel were not significant on economic issues. Instead, it was primarily political predictions (and somewhat normative evaluations) that were at the heart of the disagreements that led the panel to split fairly evenly between those who thought that some privatization was a good idea and those who thought it was not. Indeed the panel had been constructed to have that breakdown *ex ante*. What the panel experience did was to distinguish the common elements of analysis (pretty much all of positive economics) from those that separated the two camps (primarily political prognostication). Political economy is critical, even if we are only in the early stages of bringing together political and economic outcomes on a scientific basis.

These pages discuss all of the issues mentioned above, and more.

Chapter 1   Social Security Policy

Social security reform is a hot topic in many countries around the world. As usual in democracies, there are two related discussions or debates. One is a debate among politicians and policy analysts trying to influence public opinion. Second is a conversation among academics and other policy analysts. The analysts' discussion has three components: first, an attempt to communicate the elements on which analysts agree; second, research to further understanding of the economics of alternative reforms; and third and most contentious, analyses of the connection between reform proposals and possible political actions. In this chapter, I want to emphasize primarily the first and third components of the analysts' conversation. In the next two chapters, I will discuss research findings and research gaps, relating social security to the labor and capital markets.

While much economic analysis is widely applicable, political analyses vary more by country. Since it is the US political debate with which I am familiar, I hope you will excuse my need to use examples from that debate. On the side of economic analysis, I will use recent reforms in Sweden as examples to be analyzed, but I will not analyze the reforms in full detail.[1]

First, a little background on my view of the overall picture. To a large extent, the debates to reform social security are triggered by population aging and the pressure that aging puts on social security systems, particularly on defined benefit systems with little funding. This demographic pressure comes from two sources—one is the baby-boom phenomenon—for example, in Sweden, the ratio of the over-65 population to that 16–64 has gone from 0.184 in 1950 to 0.278 last year, and is projected to reach

A shorter version of this lecture has appeared in Swedish, Diamond 2000*b*.

[1] The reforms here were pending when this lecture was given and have since been implemented. Since it is too soon to evaluate the workings of the new system, I will add only a little to what was originally presented.

0.35 by 2050. The second source is the ongoing trend to lower mortality rates, which is expected to extend well into the future. This trend is a source of difficulty for any social security system, while the approaching retirement of the baby-boomers makes the issues much more pressing.

A second element that I keep in mind when considering long-term issues is that early retirement is a normal good—richer societies want more of it, *ceteris paribus*. Moreover, the relative cost of leisure activities has been falling (Costa, 1998). The very long-term trend to earlier retirement is evident in labor force participation rates of men in many countries. While social security affects retirement decisions, this trend antedates social security systems and has additional causes. Labor force participation rates of women, however, also reflect the revolution in the roles available to women in many countries and so do not show the same trend over recent decades. But for the long haul, I expect that eventually women will also exhibit an increasing popularity of early retirement.

Debates about social security reform center around two issues that are economically unrelated, although sometimes they may be politically related. One is whether to increase the extent of funding of social security, and if so, how much. The policy analysis community generally favors more funding, and I will say a few words about that. Sweden has gone down the route of eventually having more funding by dedicating 2.5 percentage points of the payroll tax to funded individual accounts, although this has been accompanied by some cutback in the partial funding of the rest of the system. The second central issue is the extent of the use of defined contribution (DC) accounts as opposed to defined benefit (DB) accounts. On this issue the policy analysis community is divided and the discussion is often heated, with disputes centering on the political implications of the alternative approaches. Sweden has chosen to introduce funded DC accounts along with a very interesting DB variant—a defined benefit system that has more automatic adjustments than is standard and moreover is couched in the vocabulary of a defined contribution system. Indeed, it is referred to as a notional defined contribution (NDC) system.

In addition to these two central elements of the debate, there are a myriad of details worthy of analysis and sometimes subject to considerable debate. After discussing funding and the contrast between DB and DC pensions in general terms, I will touch on two issues of particular relevance here—the details of organizing access to alternative portfolios for a DC system and the structure of benefits within the family, particularly the protection of elderly widows.

1.1. Funding

Let me start with the funding issue. Populations are aging. Without large changes in retirement ages, there must be a trend of rising taxes and/or declining annual benefits. Adding more funding to a system can reduce this trend, although funding at levels that are politically plausible does not change the direction of the trend, just the magnitude. Increased funding can finance part of benefits out of the excess of the rate of return over the rate of growth times the level of funds. This financing helps to lower future taxes for any level of benefits (or vice versa). But funds do not appear from nowhere—they can come from currently raising taxes, cutting benefits or finding some other source of revenue (which would have an alternative use). Raising taxes now in order to have lower taxes in the future reduces the trend toward higher taxes. So the purpose of funding is to increase the burden on current generations in order to lower the burden on future generations. This outcome is similar to that from a decision to raise taxes or cut spending in order to decrease the public debt. (Provided, of course, that the cut in spending is not a cut in public investment.) Economists see advantages in smoothing tax rates and foresee large tax increases in the future and so generally favor more funding, although there is considerable disagreement on how much.

Economists recognize that there are two aspects to increased funding, both of which matter. One is the growth of national capital and the other is the fiscal position of social security. Greater growth of national capital increases resources available in the future; a stronger fiscal position for social security affects the political process, which will determine how costs and benefits will be allocated across different cohorts in the future. So funding that is associated with increased national savings is what economists tend to favor, not funding that is merely relabeling or shuffling of liabilities. To this end, increased funding within social security should not be offset by larger government deficits out-side social security.

Economists also recognize that the real gain from increased funding is a change in intergenerational distribution; that a widely-made argument for funded individual accounts is bogus. Let me present and correct that argument. Some analysts and politicians compare the long-run return on assets with the long-run return in a pay-as-you-go (PAYG) system, which, as is well known, is the rate of growth. Since long-run rates of return are expected to exceed rates of growth, this is sometimes presented as a pure gain. But it is wrong to analyze policy by considering only the long run, not including the short-run costs and benefits asso-ciated with going to a different long run. It would be wrong to say that having the rate of interest exceed the rate of growth implies that a funded system is better. Once the analysis is done fully, incorporating both short- and long-run effects, then it is seen that there is no Pareto gain available from funding *per se*, just an inter-generational redistribution (Breyer, 1989).

The nature of this argument can be seen by considering the infin-ite horizon present-discounted-value budget constraint for social security. Defining benefits in terms of individual accounts does not change this constraint *per se*, although creating individual accounts may be bundled with benefit cuts. The constraint can be changed by raising revenues or lowering benefits. So, taking some social security revenues and moving them into individual accounts leaves behind a revenue gap that must be filled. Com-bining the need to fill this revenue gap with the other effects of creating the accounts leaves the present-discounted-value con-straint roughly unchanged. The higher rate of interest minus the extra taxes yields the rate of growth as before. This simple arithmetic is altered to the extent that the rate of return on assets can be changed. But whether individual accounts raise or lower the rate of return on assets is a complex economic and political question.

Some people have argued that a Pareto gain is available by bundling analysis of static efficiency improvements in social security together with increased funding. That is, if you find a way to make a Pareto gain within a period, that gain can be com-bined with something that is purely redistributive, and still leave everyone better off, as long as the redistribution is small enough.

But those short-run gains are available without increased funding, so this is a misattribution, unless it really is the case that the short-run gains are not available politically without such bundling. In politics bundling does matter, but such bundling, at least at this stage of the debate in the US, is not necessary for reform.

If more funding is wanted, there are multiple alternatives. Funding can be in government bonds or in a diversified portfolio. Funding can be in a central fund controlled by a government agency or in individual accounts controlled by individual workers. And realized returns on funding can affect retirement benefits in a wide variety of ways. The central gain from funding, that of accumulating resources to benefit future cohorts, is similar whichever route one takes. While portfolio diversification can be done with or without individual DC accounts, putting the choice of portfolio in the hands of workers makes little sense unless workers bear a large fraction of the consequences of such choices. I will discuss portfolio diversification in detail in lecture three; by and large, portfolio diversification appears to be a plus.

The presence of many available routes to building a diversified fund is not just a theoretical option, since different countries have gone down different routes. Funding a central diversified portfolio within a DB system has been done in Sweden for years (and will continue in a buffer stock) and it is being done in Canada and Switzerland and has been proposed by the finance minister in Ireland and the Clinton administration in the US. Funding with a central fund within a DC system happens with the provident funds of Malaysia and Singapore. And funding can be done with worker choice over portfolios made available by private providers within a DC system, as was pioneered in Chile and followed in other Latin American countries, implemented in the UK, and recently begun in Sweden. Thus, choices of a level of funding and of a degree of portfolio diversification are economically unrelated to the choice between DB and DC systems.

1.2. DB and DC

Before comparing DB and DC systems, let me give the definitions I will use. A DB system is one that has a benefit formula that relates annuitized benefits to the history of earnings covered by social security. Allowing a lump sum to replace some or all of the annuitized benefit is a minor wrinkle from this abstract perspective. The annuitized benefit might be a single-life or joint-life annuity. Indeed how alternative systems would treat women is a significant part of the debate in the US. More significant in the historic workings of DB systems is that benefits are based on earnings subject to tax, not taxes paid. Since systems have commonly had significantly increasing tax rates over time, this has been part of the mechanism that transferred large amounts to the early cohorts. For mature systems that are not anticipating much more in the way of tax increases, this dimension is of much less importance today.

A DC system is one that mandates contributions, accumulates resources in individual accounts based on actual rates of return on portfolios, and then converts the accumulated account value to a benefit stream through some combination of annuitization, lump-sum availability, and restricted monthly withdrawals. There are a host of differences between well-designed examples of DB and DC systems. One of the important ones is the focus of attention—DB systems focus attention on benefits relative to the history of earnings; DC systems focus attention on taxes paid, and so also on redistributions. In democratic societies, this difference in focus, in framing in the vocabulary of cognitive psychology, can have an important effect on political outcomes.

I want to digress for a moment to relate this difference to some of the writings of Erik Lindahl. In public finance, Lindahl is best known for his important analysis of benefit-based taxation and its role in determining public spending (1919, translated into English, 1958). If we consider pensions from this perspective, then DC accounts, without any redistribution, are an example of benefit-based taxation, except for the redistributions inherent in uniform annuitization. That is, during the accumulation phase of a DC pension, there is the direct link that the recipient of a pension pays for the financing of the account. However, when an accumulation is converted into an annuity using a conversion factor that does not vary with individual life expectancy, then a DC pension ceases to be an example of benefit-based taxation. Since higher income men tend to live longer than lower income men, this phase of a DC pension system tends to redistribute from low earners to high earners. Of course, the redistributive aspects of portions of a pension system need to be viewed within the context of the entire system. Entire systems may also contain taxation above the level that is credited for benefits, may contain a flat DB benefit to supplement the DC, and may contain a minimum benefit provision.

It is important to remember that, like Wicksell (1896, translated into English, 1958), Lindahl considered that benefit-based taxation was just only if income distribution were just. From this essential caveat, together with Lindahl's analysis of benefit-based taxation, the important next step for public finance was the writing of Richard Musgrave (1959). Musgrave separated government budgeting into three budgets, one for allocation, one for distribution, and one for stabilization. While practitioners have never lost sight of the stabilization role of public finance, the academic public finance literature has seen it pretty much disappear. Building on the writings of Musgrave, which put public finance on a sound general-equilibrium footing, has been the development of general-equilibrium second-best theories, which have advanced our understanding of both redistribution and efficient public spending, while recognizing the incentive effects of taxation. And that is how I approach social security in this book—recognizing the inevitable intertwining of incentives, insurance, and redistribution.

Lindahl's writings remind us of the importance both of recognizing beneficiaries when designing taxes and of the need for redistribution. In the absence of lump-sum taxation to provide a just income distribution, and in the absence of any other practical fiscal tools that relate to an entire history of earnings, it is important to do a good job of incorporating income distribution concerns into social security systems. Such concerns go beyond merely contributing to the reduction of poverty and include concerns about the adequacy of replacement rates at different levels of income and different stages in post-retirement family structure. The Swedish Ministry of Health and Social Affairs has recognized both issues as well, recognizing two separate goals of pension policy—to alleviate poverty among the elderly and to ease the decline of living standards as people age. It is important to recognize that these are different objectives, both of which are espoused by governments, even though some analysts view only the former as having a legitimate government role.

The distinction between DB and DC systems relative to income distribution is primarily one of politics not economics. One can set up a DB system with little *ex ante* income redistribution (apart from that inherent in uniform annuitization). An example is what are called cash-balance plans in the US—systems where individual deposits are given a fixed rate of return and then converted into annuities, independent of the returns on actual assets that may be funding the system. Conversely, one can build redistribution into a DC system. But the key political question is whether the choice of approach will affect the degree and method of redistribution. This is particularly an issue in systems, like that in Chile and proposed by some for the US, where the entire system is made a DC system (along with just a safety net). And it is an issue in Sweden, where the NDC system is described with a DC vocabulary.

This likely distinction in outcomes is widely recognized. Indeed, some have argued that DC systems are more transparent than DB systems and therefore more democratic. There are issues in pension design where alternative institutions do differ primarily in transparency—the extent to which information is made available and salient. However, in contrasting DB and DC systems generally, it seems to me that the right vocabulary is that of framing, not of transparency. As we know from cognitive psychology, particularly the work of Kahneman and Tversky (e.g. chapters in Kahneman *et al.*, 1982), framing has a very powerful effect on thought. It is not surprising that it also has a powerful effect on political outcomes. Thus, DB and DC systems vary in the focus of what is transparent, not in the presence or absence of transparency.

Defined contribution systems make the financing of benefits particularly salient, including making redistribution particularly salient. However, DC systems make the outcomes opaque, where outcomes can be measured by benefit levels relative to some measure of needs (replacement rates, measured in some way). Benefits depend on the returns on assets (which are stochastic and without anyone knowing fully the stochastic process) and on the pricing of annuities (which is also stochastic and also without anyone knowing fully the process for mortality trends). But, it is not just that individuals find it hard to tell what benefits they will receive conditional on future earnings. Also, the pattern of outcomes across different individuals is opaque. And citizens care about the pattern of incomes within a cohort.

In contrast, DB systems make individual annual benefits and benefit patterns visible, conditional, of course, on future earnings. That is, a DB system makes clear the outcomes of the system in terms of what the retirement income system is trying to do—which is to replace lost earnings. While DB systems will be adjusted from time to time, so actual benefits are stochastic, that adjustment takes place in the context of the salience of the benefit pattern. But DB systems make the connection between individual financing and individual benefits opaque. So the framing coming from the choice of the type of pension system and from the vocabulary used to describe it will affect the nature of the redistribution that is adopted.

The contrast in outcomes between public DB and DC systems also occurs in corporate pension systems. Giving past-service credits to long-term employees was common when DB systems were being set up in the US. Giving analogous lump sums to similarly placed employees when setting up DC systems has certainly been rare in the US—I have not heard of a single example, although my search has not been exhaustive. This suggests the importance of the framing done by the vocabulary used to describe a pension system.

This tension is not unique to the provision of pensions. Every government expenditure has a benefit side and a cost side. While both sides are relevant for policy, no one has found a magical government institution that gives just the right salience to the two sides. The earmarking of payroll-tax revenues for pension benefits changes the visibility of financing and the distribution of cost-bearing, and so changes political outcomes. In contrast, pension benefits for Union Army veterans from the US Civil War were financed by tariff revenues. So supporters of these pensions were big fans of trade protection. Most analysts believe that the government spends too much on some programs and too little on other programs, although analysts disagree about which programs are which. Since different government institutions (both political and administrative) lead to different outcomes and analysts evaluate outcomes differently, it is not surprising that analysts evaluate institutions differently.

It is interesting to consider the analog in medical benefits in a country like the US, which is so backward that it provides universal health insurance only to the elderly, through the Medicare program. As a DB system, Medicare can be described as giving everyone the same health insurance policy, with financing coming from payroll tax and general revenues. What if we think about Medicare as a payroll-tax financed DC system? We could describe it then as follows. Everyone is forced to save for his or her retirement medical expenses. Then, there are transfers from high to low earners, from healthy to sick and from short-lived to long-lived, in order to give each person an amount to finance covered medical expenses. This description does not seem to be more transparent, just focused on different issues. It risks losing sight of the apparent purpose of the system, which is to provide everyone with the same health insurance. It might result in a different uniform health insurance policy and it might result in transfers that do not give everyone the same insurance policy. It might result in more funding and less use of PAYG.

So too, individual pension accounts hide how the system provides income relative to past earnings. There is a tradeoff— making some aspects more salient tends to make others less salient. Maybe highlighting who pays for redistribution is most important. It seems to me that highlighting who has how much relative to their past earnings is highlighting what the system is, in its own terms, trying to do. In the US, there are individual account proposals that eliminate all redistribution in the system, except that coming from uniform annuity pricing. It is not accidental that people who oppose redistribution favor individual accounts—it would be hard to be taken seriously in the US if one proposed simply to remove progressivity from the Social Security benefit formula.

In democracies, salience affects outcomes. The real question is how much one expects to like the political outcomes that come from different institutions. So the question here is to evaluate the different patterns of redistribution, within and across cohorts, that come with different pension institutions. The common wisdom is that DC systems are likely to give more to future generations and DB systems are likely to give more to the poor within each cohort. If true (and the pattern may be more complex since DC pensions automatically cut benefits for longer-lived future cohorts, and DB systems include additional distinctions that affect benefits), which is more important? The answer depends on how well any particular country will implement the two types of redistribution under the two different institutions. It depends on what other institutions affect incomes of the elderly. For example, Argentina combines individual accounts with a DB system giving flat benefits, similar to the basic pension in Sweden in the old system. In contrast, Chile has a guaranteed minimum pension, similar to the guarantee in Sweden in the new system. By switching from a flat benefit to a guaranteed minimum, Sweden is changing the nature of redistribution—these approaches differ in the nature of redistributional intent. Since there is no necessary ranking on efficiency grounds between these approaches, this change may be related to the general move to a DC vocabulary. I will say more about these contrasting approaches in the second lecture.

I want to touch briefly on comparisons between DB and DC systems, comparisons that I will discuss in more detail in the next two lectures. First, there are no necessary advantages to DC systems in giving good incentives for the retirement decision— DB systems can make retirement benefits available with or without retirement. DB systems can imitate the way DC systems have an actuarial increase in benefits after a delayed start in benefits. Second, it is not clear which is more efficient for labor supply and earnings risk of younger workers—DC systems or DB systems using a long averaging period of earnings in determining benefits.[2] DB systems that use a short averaging period (like the old DB system in Sweden) do create significant problems for the labor market. In the second lecture I will discuss the advantages of different ways of structuring these incentives.

Third, as discussed already, the level of genuine funding and of overall portfolio diversification can be similar in either system. But, fourth, there are differences relating to the risks in the returns on assets. A DC system has the ability to let different workers expose themselves to different amounts of market risk. On the other hand, a DB system has the ability to spread rate-of-return risk over future cohorts. Historically, there has been great variability in rates of return, even on a lifetime basis. These points

---

[2] For example, the US uses the thirty-five highest (wage-indexed) earnings years, although the indexing is not done after age 60, which is a poor design.

will be discussed in the third lecture, along with some of the general equilibrium effects associated with funding and portfolio choice. And, fifth, DC systems that give access to a wide market for portfolio choice are considerably more expensive to administer than well-run DB systems, as I will discuss later in this lecture.

Where the systems also differ is in the way they naturally respond to the need for change, which can affect the political outcome. Consider the response to increasing life expectancy after retirement. A DC system naturally cuts benefits in response to an actuarial evaluation that retirees will collect benefits for longer. The natural response in a DB system is to need legislation in response to financial pressures generated by longer lives for retirees. While a DB system could include indexing for life expectancy, as does the NDC system in the reform here, this response is unusual for a DB system. A legislature can have a benefit formula that changes over time to reflect anticipated life expectancy as of the time of legislation. Such a change was the approach taken partially in the US in the 1983 legislation that slowly increased the "Normal Retirement Age," which is nothing more than a parameter in the determination of benefits.

With DC, benefits depend on taxes that have been paid rather than earnings that have been subject to tax. With a stable tax rate, this difference is not an important one. Nevertheless, the difference can affect legislation in the event of future changes to the system. As an example, consider what might happen if it is decided to increase the tax rate and the benefit level because it was decided that a larger system was better, perhaps because people were living longer and replacement rates were judged to be too low. With a DC approach, the increase in the tax rate would eventually increase benefits as those who paid higher taxes started to receive benefits. Those already retired when taxes increase would not receive a benefit increase unless there was an explicit transfer, separate from the increase in the tax rate. And the size of benefit increase would vary across cohorts with their age at the time of the legislated change in the tax rate.

In contrast, with a system based on earnings subject to tax (but otherwise the same) a tax rate increase would permit the legislature to phase-in a benefit increase across all cohorts, in a way that satisfied the same present-discounted-value budget constraint as in the DC case. Plausibly, early cohorts, possibly including the already retired, would receive more than with the DC framework, while later cohorts would receive less.

There are two dimensions to how the natural DB outcome would differ from its DC counterpart. One, the dimension highlighted by the DC approach is that there would be intergenerational redistribution toward earlier generations with DB. The other, highlighted by the DB approach, is that the movement to a more appropriate level of benefits would be shared among cohorts with DB. Both of these aspects of the difference in likely outcomes are relevant for policy choice. And it is not obvious which one would give a better outcome. Indeed one would expect that an outside observer would vary the ranking of the outcomes depending on such things as differences in the relative well-being of different cohorts and the pattern of redistribution already in place. And the ranking would vary with differences in political predictions about future legislation.

In addition to intergenerational differences, there are likely to be differences in responses within a cohort, depending on how redistribution is organized. As an example, let me contrast a unified DB system with a mixed DB/DC system with roughly the same funding and the same overall redistribution to begin. If there is a decline in economic growth, then the underfunded DB benefits will need adjustment. Some of the adjustment may come from taxes. Let us focus on the adjustment that comes on the benefit side. If, for example, the mixed system combines a flat DB benefit with a nonredistributive DC system, then the response is likely to be a phased-in cut in the flat DB benefit. That is, every member of a cohort will have the same absolute cut in benefits. It seems implausible that a unified system facing the same financial problem would choose that outcome. Thus, this sort of mixed system puts more of the risk of the PAYG financing on the poor. On the other hand, if the unified DB system adjusts benefits in proportion, a mixed system would put more of the rate-of-return risk on the rich. Also, a DB system can spread rate-of-return risk over many cohorts, possibly making that risk less of a concern.

Not only do systems tend to respond differently to exogenous changes, they differ in how they generate political forces that can affect future legislation. Let me give an example affecting DC accounts. The clear message about these accounts is that the resources in an account belong to the worker. The worker controls how it is invested, with very little apparent restriction, possibly little different from voluntary accounts. The worker receives all of the benefits financed by the accounts, provided the worker survives. Will this mindset about these accounts lead to objections to the restrictions that are placed on the accounts here? The primary restrictions are on the necessity of annuitization, the form of annuitization, and the need to survive to retirement age (or transfer the money earlier) in order to receive anything from the account. All of these could well be questioned by workers who prefer to leave the money to an heir (and not just purchase life insurance), who prefer lump sums, or who want alternative forms of annuitization, all of which may not work as well from a social point of view. So, there is concern about the political sustainability of the restrictions on DC accounts. A similar issue arises for NDC accounts to the extent that they are described in similar terms.

Also relevant is whether workers will understand the differences between the NDC accounts and the funded DC accounts in Sweden. From a worker's point of view she is paying for both of them. Why then does one pay a higher rate of return than the other? Why then is one subject to more restrictions than the other? These questions can generate political pressures. These issues could have been handled differently. The NDC system is paying a lower rate of return because earlier generations of retirees received higher benefits. That is, there is an implicit liability to the continuing social security system because earlier cohorts received larger benefits than could have been financed by their taxes. From the perspective of now, that is history, and cannot be reversed. The question is how to pay for the implicit liability, just as future cohorts must pay for the national debt. The current design here allocates all of this liability to the NDC accounts and none of it to the DC accounts. It is not surprising if workers do not understand implicit liability and do not understand why the accounts are different. One approach to having better understanding would be to equalize the taxation of the two kinds of accounts. A portion of the money devoted to DC accounts could be taxed and added to the buffer stock for NDC accounts to reflect the reality of the incompleteness of the asset value of the buffer stocks. Both types of accounts could be "taxed" at the same percentage rate.

1.3. Notional Defined Contribution Accounts

I have discussed concerns about both DB and DC systems. Some of these concerns have led to proposals that are hybrids. I want to discuss the proposal that has been made by my colleague, Franco Modigliani, together with Ceprini (1998), and Ceprini and Muralidhar (2000), and also the approach that is being used in Sweden (and has been adopted in Italy, Latvia and Poland).

Modigliani and co-authors are proposing that the US and Italy structure their systems like some corporate plans, which are called cash-balance plans. Like DC plans they are funded and accumulate contributions to finance an annuity priced according to actuarial principles. But like DB plans, the intent is to move some rate-of-return risk from the individual benefit recipient to the financers of the program. In Modigliani's proposal for the US, accounts are to have a 5 percent real rate of return whatever happens to market returns, with the risk on the US Treasury. Instead, one could treat returns as with conventional DB plans, by leaving it to Congress to adjust the rate of return paid on accounts and the tax rate in response to realized returns. While one could include redistribution across accounts as part of such a system (and Modigliani favors doing so), a critical issue is the extent to which the political process would indeed do so.

Compared with a similarly financed standard DB system, the political argument in favor of this approach is that there are "ownership" rights to the individual accounts, thereby lessening the possibility that the funds would be used by the government for other purposes. On the other hand, there could be an impact decreasing redistributions to the poor. Compared with a similarly financed DC system, the economic argument in favor of this approach is that the rate-of-return risks from funding are spread more widely. This risk allocation affects both *ex ante* risk from an individual perspective and the diversity of pension benefits for workers with similar past earnings, who might have differed in portfolio choice or timing of accumulation and retirement. On the other hand, it has the disadvantage of a provident fund system that there is not diversity in risk sharing within a cohort. By determining monthly benefits by actuarial pricing, given the accumulation in an account, this approach, like DC accounts, automatically cuts benefits for cohorts that have longer life expectancy. It also relates benefits to taxes paid, not earnings subject to tax and, relates benefits to all contributions, weighting contributions in different years according to the legislated real interest rate. These latter aspects do not differ greatly from the current US system that uses thirty-five years of earnings, expects a fairly stable tax rate, and weights annual earnings by the growth in an average earnings index.

The NDC system here takes a different approach. It is designed to be an unfunded system (with a buffer stock of assets) that uses automatic adjustments to preserve financial stability, rather than relying on legislative actions.[3] Let me turn to the issue of automatic adjustments in DB systems.

One could have a DB system with benefit determination fully described in nominal terms. Indeed, that was the system in the US prior to 1972. However, it is widely recognized that a system defined wholly in nominal terms has a poor design. In order to serve as a reasonably reliable source of reasonably determined retirement benefits, systems are typically indexed in some form to prices and/or wages, both to decrease the frequency of legislative interventions and to fix expectations that will affect the interventions that do occur.[4] The NDC approach goes further by adjusting benefits to cohort life expectancy and by indexing both the accumulation parameter in the benefit formula and the growth of benefits after retirement to an index of earnings growth, since earnings growth is central to the financing of a PAYG system. Recognizing that labor force growth as well as average earnings growth are important for financing, there is also a fall-back adjustment, if needed, to growth of total, rather than average, taxable earnings.[5]

The accumulation of values in accounts using a wage growth index is common to DB systems and will not be discussed. I will consider the adjustment of initial benefits for life expectancy, the

---

[3] "Strictly speaking, pension rights relate to pensionable income, not to total paid-in contributions." Ministry of Health and Social Affairs, The Pension Reform in Sweden, Final Report, June 1998, p. 24.

[4] Countries that are adjusting pension benefits as part of an annual budget cycle have not succeeded in setting up a reliable pension system.

[5] Average earnings growth differs from the growth of payroll tax revenue not only from the growth of the labor force but also, to a lesser extent, by the distribution of earnings.

adjustment of benefits in payment by a wage index, and the adjustment of accounts for realized mortality experience before retirement.[6]

This NDC system adjusts benefits for life expectancy at the time a cohort reaches the age at which benefits can be claimed (without disability). A standard DB system uses a benefit formula that is not related to life expectancy. A legislature could have a benefit formula that changes over cohorts to reflect anticipated life expectancy, as was done in the US in the 1983 legislation. The idea of lowering benefits for longer-lived cohorts as a way of limiting cost does seem appropriate. However, I question the approach of the NDC system that does 100 percent of the adjustment to longer lives on the side of benefits and zero on the side of taxes. Indeed, it appears that preserving the tax rate may have been an overriding goal.

The trend to longer lives should continue through the upcoming century and requires some adaptation inside and outside social security. Unless workers save more or retire later, they will have less per month in retirement. A sensible adaptation would have some of all three—more savings, longer work, and lower retirement spending, unless the current system is considered too large and the NDC approach is primarily a politically acceptable way to shrink it.

Social security itself does not require anyone to retire at any age. After eligibility to claim benefits here at age 61, a worker can start receiving benefits, or can wait and receive larger benefits that start later. Thus, social security allows workers to adapt to longer lives by working longer for larger monthly benefits. The incentives for delaying retirement beyond the earliest age of eligibility will play an important part in determining just when workers retire, and so the impact on monthly benefits of longer lives. But of the other two adaptations—lower monthly benefits and higher savings, the adaptation is completely on lower benefits, without any currently legislated or automatically adjusting increases in future payroll-tax rates. Indeed the NDC approach seems to take avoidance of pressure to increase taxes as the single overriding goal of system design. It seems to me that this

---

[6] Annuities in payment could also be adjusted for mortality as is done by CREF annuities (Valdés-Prieto, 1998).

approach loads too much of the response to increased life expectancy onto benefit cuts.

Let me briefly consider the other two elements. The use of a wage index for benefits in payment places some of wage growth risk on retirees. Use of a price index, or a combination of the two indices, is a device for placing less risk on retirees. Finance principles suggest that retirees should bear some of the wage growth risk. This principle is reinforced by relative income concerns, especially since some retirees will live a long time. But retirees are less able to bear risk than younger workers, suggesting that the NDC rule may involve too much risk on retirees. The use here of deviations from 1.6 percent wage growth to determine benefit growth is simply a device for tilting the benefit stream over time. Similarly, the use of a different index, together with a different initial benefit, can be done in a revenue neutral way in expected value. Less tight indexing of benefits to revenues leaves more risk that legislation might be needed. But, avoiding new legislation is not an absolute, but should be balanced with the risks falling on the elderly.

The values in accounts of workers who die before retirement will be redistributed within a single-year age cohort. A standard DB system similarly leaves no money for the estates of those dying before retirement (although there may also be life insurance and survivors benefits within the system). With the NDC approach here, the redistribution from the lack of estates goes to other members of the same cohort, rather than being spread more widely as with a standard DB system.

1.4. Organizing DC Accounts

A country deciding to have funded individual DC accounts has many options on how to organize the accumulation phase of these accounts. The simplest solution is to have the government select the portfolios for the individual accounts. This can be done with everyone holding the same portfolio, as in Singapore and Malaysia, referred to as a provident fund. The economic advantage of this approach is that it minimizes the administrative costs of organizing the portfolio; indeed, the costs should not differ much from those arising from investing a fund for a DB system (just a need to track overall values more frequently). The economic shortcoming is that everyone holds the same portfolio, even though consideration of risk bearing suggests that different people should hold different portfolios. The importance of this issue varies with the size of the portfolio and the extent of savings outside the system, since it is the makeup of total portfolios that matters. For many people the exact portfolio choice within social security may not matter (as long as it is efficient). Shortcomings in the stock–bond mix of the social security portfolio can be offset by complementary changes on the balance of an individual's portfolio. Of course this option is not available when people have little in the way of financial assets outside the system. In theory, and I suspect in practice, one can do better by having the government choose different portfolios based on age—for example, with a balance between stock and bond index funds shifting toward less risk as people age. Perhaps one could find additional easily measured variables that could be used to differentiate portfolios.

While analysts disagree on the economic importance of having a wide array of choices for workers, the heart of the debate in the US is on the politics of portfolio choice. The political issue is how well the government would select a portfolio, particularly if it is for a DB system. This is made up of two parts—whether the government will select a portfolio on the risk-return frontier and what trade-off between risk and return it will choose. In the widely read World Bank book (1994), *Averting the Old Age Crisis*, the poor performance of some governments in investing centralized funds was highlighted. However, many of the countries cited have governments that don't function well on many dimensions and capital markets that offer poor choices to everyone. So one needs caution in deciding for which countries this message is important. Moreover, there has been progress in the ability of governments to invest well. In the US, the evidence (Munnell and Sundén, 1999) is that state and local governments are doing better than earlier with their diversified portfolios. Recently, they have done as well as privately managed portfolios, and even in the past, the magnitude of the problems was not enormous. More generally, one would expect the wide development and use of index funds to make this problem much easier. However, the feasibility of heavy reliance on index funds depends on social security funds not being too large relative to the capital market.

It will be interesting in the future to compare risks and returns on the Swedish NDC buffer stock, which is centrally run, with the returns on individual accounts.

If one wants to move the decision about portfolios away from the government and to individuals, there are various ways to organize the alternatives. Before turning to alternative approaches, let me comment on allowing choice at all. Presumably the politics of portfolio choice change as we move from a DB fund to a centralized DC fund. However, choices will be regulated and one needs to recognize that the politics of the regulation of portfolios has its own potential shortcomings as well as the politics of direct government portfolio choice.

An obvious economic disadvantage to worker choice is that administrative costs go up. I will say more about this as we consider the costs with alternative organizational modes. In addition, individual choices will vary in a way that a centralized formula would not duplicate. Is this likely to be good or bad? My answer is some of both, with the balance waiting to be better informed by more research on individual portfolio choice. That is, some individuals will choose well (in an *ex ante* sense) given their degree of risk aversion and given the risk-return frontier that is made available. Others will choose badly—both choosing points that are not on the frontier or choosing points that are not appropriate given their risk aversion. After all, understanding the principles of finance is not simple. The advantages of diversification, the concept of a risk-return trade-off, the difficulty of inferring underlying stochastic structures, and the risks in attempting to time markets are not intuitively simple concepts. Indeed, cognitive psychology tells us that statistical properties are not intuitive, even much simpler concepts than those needed to understand portfolio choice. Moreover, given the noise in returns, it is difficult for anyone to tell good portfolio managers from bad ones. Studying mutual funds in Sweden, Dahlquist *et al.* (1999: p. 2) "find little evidence of persistence in performance." And with some organizational structures, efforts to prevent fraud and mis-selling will be extremely important. The "mis-selling scandal" in the UK reminds us of this issue (Gillion *et al.*, 2000, pp. 320–4).

What do we actually know about individual choice? Some, but not as much as I would like. There have been studies of the choices people make in employer-provided DC plans in the US, called 401(k) plans. There are also studies that look at total portfolio holdings. The simple summary is that while broad averages tend to move in the directions that finance theory suggests is sensible (Bodie and Crane, 1997), some people invest nothing in stocks and some invest completely in stocks, and it is likely that a significant fraction are not making really good choices.[7] For example, many people invest heavily in the stock of their own employer—probably showing limited understanding of the advantages of diversification—both across stocks and in the combination of earnings and asset returns. In addition, many people who choose individual stocks appear to trade too much—lowering the combination of risk and return after trades, on average, as well as incurring trading costs (Odean and Barber, 2000). There is suggestive evidence that individuals do less well than the funds in which they invest (Dalbar, 1993), presumably from people trying to time the market, moving between classes of assets in a way that increases risk relative to expected return and seems to lower expected return on average as well. As in consumer markets generally, people choose products at higher costs than seemingly identical products also available in the market.

So there is a strong basis to be skeptical about the gains from individual choice *per se*. Will learning-by-doing take care of that? The evidence suggests not. In the US, experience with worker education in 401(k) plans shows that substantial and expensive worker education is needed to have a noticeable effect on workers' investment choices (Bayer *et al.*, 1996).

Deciding to have individual choice still leaves alternative approaches to organizing the market. If one wanted to have individual choice from a limited menu of alternatives, one can do this most cheaply by having the government organize the accounts. That is, let the government select a limited set of alternatives for workers. The centerpiece of such an approach is bidding by providers for a limited number of places in this set of

---

[7] Bodie and Crane find that the proportion of holdings in stock increases with wealth and decreases with age, both in line with financial advice. This is a not uncommon outcome in economic research using rational agent theory. While the theory correctly predicts the signs of cross-section patterns of behavior, it fails to some degree at predicting the levels. Bodie and Crane do find that portfolio choice inside and outside tax-favored retirement accounts does not minimize tax burden.

alternatives.[8] This approach of government-organized accounts is done best with a separation of recordkeeping and communication from management of investment, as is being done here.[9] This approach is in contrast to having a privately organized market, where a wide array of private providers determine what is available in the market (subject, of course, to regulation) and individuals choose providers, not just portfolios.[10]

In the US, the model for this approach is the Thrift Savings Plan (TSP), a defined contribution system that the federal government provides for more than two million employees. Let me describe briefly how this works. The TSP has had three investment options—an S&P 500 index fund, and two bond funds. Individuals can spread their accounts across these three funds as they wish. TSP is in the process of adding several more options. The fund managers, who were selected in a competitive bidding process, exercise the share voting rights, as do fund managers generally in the US. To date there has been no political interference in the investment process. The cost of investment management is tiny, about one basis point (1/100th of 1 percent) of assets under management each year. Total costs are also small—on the order of $20 per person per year. Investment management is roughly 10 percent of total costs. However, in considering how low total costs are, it is worth recognizing that the monthly deposits come electronically from a single employer and the retail level of providing information to workers is handled and paid for by the employing federal agencies, not the TSP. Indeed the TSP does not even have a toll-free telephone number. Moreover, on average, federal employees are better educated and have more access to inexpensive communication (the internet) than the American public generally. That is why I estimated that expanding the TSP

---

[8] With this approach individuals get to choose portfolios, but they do not get to choose providers (including a lack of choice of provider even if the government uses multiple providers of similar portfolios).

[9] Without separation, there is a further complication arising from the necessary incompleteness in the contract as to the level of services to be provided—ease of access to information, speed and accuracy of record-keeping and investment, frequency of allowable changes. There will always be tension here, requiring oversight for the level of provided services. How well a government can handle these chores—selection of portfolios, selection of providers and oversight of providers, is a critical element in judging how well such a system will work.

[10] This distinction between organizing principles is discussed at length in Diamond 1999*a*.

approach to the entire US population, with a politically plausible level of services, would cost roughly twice as much per person per year as does the TSP (Diamond, 2000*a*).[11]

One plus of this approach is that it pretty much eliminates the profit-oriented advertising to workers. I can't help but notice how little information content is in the television ads that I see in the US from different investment companies. A centralized approach has a negative side in that workers might get too little information, as has been the case with Social Security in the US, where annual statements should have been instituted long ago. There is also the issue of how well the selection process for providers will work. This approach puts the issues of potential corruption, collusion, and rent-seeking in the center. The scope for good selection is likely to be affected by whether this is the only institutional pricing in the country or whether there are other (private and public) uses of this organizational approach to serve as a benchmark.

In contrast with this centralized approach, there is the approach of privately-organized markets. This approach is meant to give workers access to a wide array of choices, with the design of the choices done by the market, subject to strict regulation. The basic intent is easy entry for potential competitors, relying on competition not regulation to hold down costs and to make choices attractive. This is the approach that was taken by Chile, although they implemented some rate of return guarantees that have had the effect of severely limiting the actual range of choices. It is also the approach that has been taken by the Latin American imitators of Chile.

A market with a wide choice of mutual funds does not behave like an idealized competitive market. Individuals are somewhat responsive to differences in price and quality, but that responsiveness is limited in both size and speed. In a setting like this, the pressure on pricing from consumer responses is present but limited. We would expect to find equilibrium with prices above marginal costs, with advertising to attract profitable customers, and with a wide range of prices for similar or identical products.

---

[11] Similarly, the costs of funded DB systems can be very small. The US Social Security has a cost of roughly $10 per person per year for both accumulation and benefit payment (but excluding the disability program, which is inherently more expensive because of the need to check on disability status.) This is in line with many other programs in advanced countries.

Indeed these properties hold for all consumer markets. We can ask about the importance of these properties relative to other consumer markets. And we can consider how different types of regulation might change a market with these properties.

Several elements stand out. A mandated market aiming at everyone will include a large number of inexperienced investors. It will include a large number of low-earners, many of whom will have intermittent covered employment and all of whom will have small accounts. At a minimum, this raises the issue of the distributional implications of alternative ways of allocating the costs of running the accounts. Also those with small balances will have little incentive to monitor their accounts closely. Little monitoring will also be done by some because of their limited attention to retirement issues, and by others because of the presence of income guarantees once they do retire. Procrastination in reconsidering portfolio providers may be particularly rampant (O'Donoghue and Rabin, 1999)—there is little apparent gain from changing providers this month rather than next month, even if one had the ability to tell good providers from bad ones. And the great stochastic variability in returns makes it hard to tell good providers from bad ones. The difficulty in evaluating providers of financial services is further complicated when the pricing structure is complex, as was the case, for example, in the UK market for opt-out pensions.

In this setting, there are likely to be pluses and minuses to different regulations. Regulations might require uniform pricing, as opposed to allowing workers to form groups and bargain for reduced rates.[12] Regulations might require uniformity of pricing in percentage terms, to enhance cross subsidization of low earners. Regulations might restrict the allowable structure of pricing. Chile restricts prices to front loads and the UK market has suffered from the complexity of pricing, which is hard for workers to understand.

In the absence of a well-developed industrial organization theory of such mandated markets, we can turn to various mandatory and voluntary markets for insight into costs. In Chile, the only

---

[12] Nonuniform pricing might lower costs for some workers while raising it for others. I suspect that the total costs of the system are not theoretically comparable in general, but that theory has not been worked out.

allowable cost is a front load of roughly 15 percent on average for all deposits. A front load reduces final accumulations by the same percentage. That is, benefits are 15 percent lower than they would be if these costs could be avoided. In other Latin American countries, where accounts are smaller, the front load is larger in percentage terms. That costs are higher in percentage terms for smaller accounts is a cautionary point for the accounts here, which are based on only 2.5 percent of earnings.

In the UK with a complex pricing structure, we need a way to combine the variety of charges into a single measure of total costs. One method is to consider the loss in accumulations at retirement (compared with an account with no charges) for a worker who had a 40-year career and faced the "average" structure of charges. The percentage loss in final balances as a result of administrative charges is called the charge ratio. Murthi *et al.* (1999) find a charge ratio above one-third in the UK for the accumulation phase (including the costs from the typical pattern of transferring among providers), not counting annuitization costs. That is, benefits are one-third less than they would be if these costs could be avoided.

In the US there are analyses of the voluntary mutual fund industry. For 1998, Rea *et al.* (1999) find charges of 109 basis points for bond mutual funds and 135 basis points for equity mutual funds. This calculation includes annual fees and an annualization of front loads based on the average length of holding of such accounts. It does not include brokerage charges for transactions by the funds. Nor does it reflect the fact that many US investors pay separately for investment advice, sometimes as much as 1 percent of assets in what are called wrap accounts. Dahlquist *et al.* (1999) report annual charges of 1.5 percent on equity mutual funds and 0.7 percent on bond mutual funds in Sweden, although these calculations do not include front loads.

Converting such annual charges on balances into lifetime losses at retirement, a 1 percent per year charge on balances gives a charge ratio of roughly 20 percent. That is, a worker paying 1 percent of balances each year would have a roughly 20 percent lower retirement benefit than if these costs could be avoided. Some find this number surprising. But a 1 percent per year charge made each year is a charge that falls on deposits roughly twenty times on average if deposits are made annually over a 40-year career.[13] The relationship is close to proportional between annual charges on balances and total loss by retirement with a factor of roughly twenty. In other words, the charges on individual accounts act like benefit cuts compared with the same investments done centrally. These costs are large, suggesting that wide choice may not be worthwhile.

Two approaches come to mind as methods to hold down costs in privately-organized accounts, since such large costs are a problem. Price sensitivity of consumers is likely to be increased by restrictions on allowable products, either directly (e.g. only bond or stock or balanced index funds) or indirectly (e.g. through the incentives from guarantees, as in Chile). Less variety in products is likely to put more attention on pricing. Of course, not all index funds using the same index are the same, but it is easier to appreciate the differences.

Also, in a setting like this, the government could try price regulation, while still trying to give workers access to a wide market with easy entrance. Regulation could take the form of price maxima by type of product. Or it could take the form of firm-by-firm negotiations to determine the pricing for a firm to be allowed in the market. Or it could take the form of a formula relating allowable charges to various elements. The latter is the approach taken here in Sweden, where roughly 500 different mutual funds are available to workers. But price regulation raises the long-standing issue of how well a government can regulate prices in the interests of consumers over the long haul. Worldwide, the record on price controls has not been terribly good. Since I interpret the Swedish approach to be in this class, I am skeptical of the ability of the Swedish approach to hold down costs in the long run. And even if successful, the costs will be considerably higher than with government-organized individual choice from a limited menu.

---

[13] For a worker with a 40-year career, exponential wage growth of 2.1% per year and a portfolio that earns 4% per year, a 1% management fee reduces the value of the account by 20%. Higher wage growth reduces the charge ratio, since more contributions are made later in the worker's career and thereby subject to the management fee for fewer years. A lower management fee reduces the charge ratio roughly proportionally over the relevant range. A shorter working career, ending at retirement, also lowers the charge ratio. But a shorter working career early in life increases the charge ratio.

In sum, privately organized individual funded accounts have been expensive. There may not be methods to successfully hold down costs for the long run significantly below the level observed in Chile—we will see with experience here over time. Government-organized accounts, with limited alternatives and bidding for the opportunities, can hold down costs significantly; but successful implementation puts significant demands on the abilities of government.

1.5. Benefits

As mentioned above, there are also multiple options for the benefit phase. There are three issues I want to consider very briefly. One is the age at which retirement benefits are first made available. Second is the use of uniform annuitization within a cohort. And third is protection of members of the family— perhaps in the form of required joint-life annuitization.[14]

The early entitlement age of 61 in Sweden is not scheduled to change. This strikes me as a reasonable balance between the likely ability of workers to work longer as health improves in the future and the likely desire of workers to retire earlier as they become wealthier. The structure of actuarial adjustment of benefits here allows workers to work longer for higher benefits. But that does not mean the minimum age for retirement benefits

---

[14] Let me quickly list some of the other features of the overall system, once it is phased in. There remains a means-tested safety net. There is a guaranteed minimum pension after age 65 with offsets against the public pension system; the amount is smoothly phased out rather than being a fixed amount. Earnings are taxed at 18.5% with an upper limit on the employee, but not the employer halves. Credit will be given for looking after children and national service and during unemployment and disability, with credits paid for as accrued by the government. Pensions may be claimed in whole or in part after age 61. The conversion of accumulations into annuities is done by a formula resembling an actuarial formula, but without anticipated mortality improvements and without weighting life expectancies by the wealth to be annuitized. The NDC pension is a single-life annuity. The DC pension allows a choice of single and joint-life pensions and also allows pre-retirement transfers between spouses.

There are a variety of ways to have different aspects of redistribution in a pension system. These include, a means-tested safety net, a progressive DB benefit formula, a redistributive DC system, taxation that falls more heavily on high earners than is credited to accounts in either DB or DC systems, or a combination of the above.

is irrelevant since life expectancies vary by person and since some people will not do a good job of planning for a potentially long future horizon. Moreover, the ability to pick the time for annuitization introduces an element of adverse selection. Those with short life expectancy will have an incentive to claim early, while those with long life expectancy will have an incentive to delay claiming. Issues like this necessarily arise because of heterogeneity in life expectancy (as I will discuss in the second lecture).

Both the NDC and DC accounts here are converted into annuities using factors that depend on age and cohort but no other factors. Yet, on average, women live longer than men. And on average high earners live longer than low earners. Thus a mandatory DC system without explicit redistribution will redistribute from men, on average, to women, on average, and within each sex, from low earners, on average, to high earners, on average. While there is considerable awareness of the difference across men and women, the difference by income level does not generally receive as much attention. It may stand as an example of how the salience of redistribution affects outcomes. In the US, the differences in life expectancy are seen as part of the justification for a progressive benefit formula.

In the prefunded DC system, joint-life annuitization (with spouses or children) is allowed at retirement, as are transfers of pension rights between spouses earlier. But these are not allowed in the PAYG NDC system. This raises two issues. One is the potential for an adverse selection element. Let us see how this could work in a simple example of a fully cooperating couple. A husband (with a shorter life expectancy) transfers all of his pension rights to his wife. In addition, a life insurance policy is taken out on her life of an amount sufficient to then buy him an annuity. If all three of the mandatory annuity, the private annuity and the life insurance policy are priced the same, then this does not matter. However, if there is a pricing difference, for example from unisex tables in the mandatory policy but separate tables in the private market, then there is an opportunity to game the system. A similar opportunity comes with the option of a joint life annuity if the husband makes such a purchase, while the wife does not (together with a purchase of life insurance on her life). Similar opportunities arise if one of the couple is in poor health. There is always an issue of greater choice having both positives and negatives when pricing is not ideal, as it never can be. This raises the issue of considering a limit on joint-life annuitization although limiting it just to the DC system does not seem ideal.

More important than the potential for gaming is the issue of treatment of a survivor relative to treatment of a couple. There are economies of scale in the living of couples. These economies are recognized in the guaranteed pension here by setting the guarantee at 2.13 base amounts for a single person and 1.90 base amounts each for members of a couple. The ratio of 0.56 for a single person relative to a couple seems low compared with studies of economies of scale.[15] Insofar as the system is concerned with maintaining living standards, an objective of the Ministry, then the provision of adequate benefits after the death of one spouse is an important issue. In the US, using panel data, Holden and Zick (1998) have found that on average, income relative to a measure of need shows a considerable drop when women are widowed. It would be interesting to see such a calculation done here. Even if husband and wife had the same earnings, the economies of scale in living suggest that a survivor should have more than one-half of the pension income. For US Social Security, the typical case has between half and two-thirds going to the survivor (subject to further complications related to age at claiming). Some analysts think that a survivor needs roughly 70 percent of what the couple had. Of course, people can take advantage of the economies of scale in living without marrying.

This issue is of further concern once we recognize that there is diversity in incomes of spouses. Insofar as a lower earning spouse is the survivor, there is a further fall in the standard of living beyond the loss of economies of scale. This fall may be further exacerbated if husband and wife chose to retire at the same time even though one of them may have been younger, and so had a larger actuarial divisor in determining his or her pension. In principle, all of this can be dealt with by the couple using other resources including the funded pension and the purchase of life insurance. But in practice, I wonder what the implications will be for the living standards of surviving spouses, who are

[15] Similarly, in the basic pension, which is being phased out, a married couple received 164% of what a single person received—or a single person received 61% of what a couple received.

predominantly women. In the US, there was a big effect from a regulation requiring a signed statement by a spouse before permitting the selection of a single-life pension from an employer. I wonder at the logic of allowing protection of a spouse in the prefunded system, but not the PAYG system. And I am surprised at this lack of intervention within the family. Sweden, like the US, provides protection for the claims of spouses in estates. I wonder if there should be similar protection for mandatory pensions.

1.6. Concluding Remarks

We have covered a great deal of ground, probably too much, and I won't attempt to recap. I did not touch on the contrast between a universal flat benefit and a guaranteed minimum benefit, which I will discuss in the second chapter. There are many ways to have good systems for providing retirement income, although many countries do poorly. The Swedish design succeeds in providing reliability and reasonable labor market incentives. But more should be done to have a better pattern of replacement rates.

Chapter 2   Social Security and the Labor Market

Social security systems have a large effect on retirement decisions (Gruber and Wise, 1999). However, since early retirement is a normal or even a luxury good, and since leisure activities, like travel, have been steadily falling in real cost, social security systems are not the only cause of the long-term trend to earlier retirement (Costa, 1998). And social security also affects earlier labor market outcomes.

This chapter considers theoretical frameworks for analyzing the impact of social security on labor supply, considering both positive and normative aspects. Particular attention will be paid to the differences arising from different design details in social security systems. The first part of the chapter focuses on retirement decisions, while the second part considers earlier labor supply decisions. My focus is on issues of good design, not a cataloging of different poor design features that are found in different countries.

The topic stands out for two reasons besides its inherent importance. First is the recognition of some behavior that is not adequately modeled by the standard rational model. Second is the central role played by incomplete markets, at least in the sense of the way in which people actually use markets. Labor market decisions are made on a rolling basis. Voluntary annuities are little used and mandatory annuitization choices, if any, are normally made available after reaching an advanced age. These are significant deviations from the Arrow–Debreu setting, and so affect normative analyses of social security, which must be approached as part of second-best theory, not as an application of the fundamental welfare theorem.

While the first chapter focused on social security systems as we find them including attention to politics, this one is about economics and more about systems as we might find them. This approach helps to separate out the long list of effects of complicated systems into component parts.

2.1. Retirement Decisions

The term retirement is used in a variety of ways. Some workers retire from a career job, often accepting a pension provided through the employer, but continuing to work full-time, simply moving to another employer. Others retire from full-time work, to take on part-time work, often referred to as a bridge job. Quinn (1997) estimates that roughly one-third of US males hold bridge jobs between full-time work and full-time retirement. Yet others move directly from full-time work to being fully out of the paid labor force or at least the taxed portion of employment. There may or may not be a spell of genuine unemployment between the end of the last full-time job and the end of active participation in the paid labor market. And some collect disability benefits between a last job and the start of retirement benefits. I will pass over these distinctions and consider only the simplest move from full-time work to being fully out of the paid labor force, referring to this as retirement and the age at which it happens as the retirement age. Even with this simplification, the discussion to follow will be complicated enough.

One further element of vocabulary. The term "retirement age" is used in a variety of inconsistent ways, including the age at which a worker stops working, the age at which a worker claims retirement benefits, the age at which a worker is first eligible for some retirement benefits, and the age at which a worker is entitled to benefits which are labeled full benefits or unreduced benefits or normal benefits. I will try to be careful to distinguish these alternative uses. I will refer to the age at which retirement benefits can first be claimed as the early or first entitlement age (EEA), distinguishing an entitlement to claim retirement benefits, as opposed to benefits related to unemployment or disability. And I will make no use of the concept of full or normal benefits, except to refer to its role in defining benefits in current US legislation. That is a concept I do not find analytically useful, although it plays a big role in public discussions and some have suggested that it may play a role as a norm for retirement decisions.

Before proceeding, let me give again the definitions presented in the first lecture. A defined benefit (DB) system is one that has a benefit formula that relates annuitized benefits to the history of earnings covered by the pension plan. Allowing a lump sum to replace some or all of the annuitized benefit is a minor wrinkle from this abstract perspective. The annuitized benefit might be a single-life annuity or joint-life. A defined contribution (DC) system is one that mandates contributions, accumulates resources in individual accounts based on actual rates of return on portfolios, and then converts the accumulated account value to a benefit stream through some combination of annuitization, lump-sum availability, and restricted monthly withdrawals. These definitions focus on part of the differences across systems, but what I take to be a critical part. Since systems are often mixed, it is the central element that defines the categorization I will use. A notional defined contribution (NDC) system is a hybrid in that it is based on taxes, and counts all of them, but accumulates using a chosen index rather than the rate of return on an actual portfolio. Annuitization may or may not be based on market principles.

2.1.1. Forced Savings

Social security is made up of two mandates—one is to pay while earning (whether called taxes or contributions) and the second is to receive benefits in a particular form. Benefits are commonly received as an annuity, but also there is a restriction that they cannot be received until some condition is satisfied. The restriction might be just age or age and retirement, with retirement measured by earnings. I will refer to such a condition for receiving benefits as an earnings test. More complex rules based on replacement rates are also possible and one is in use in Chile where earlier access to benefits is allowed for those able to finance a large enough benefit and a large enough replacement rate. It is important to recognize both mandates—the mandate to pay and the restriction on access to benefits.

Let us start by examining a setting where a fully rational worker receives back the taxes paid plus (nonstochastic) interest, with benefits starting at a given EEA, and with no other conditions. We also ignore uncertainty about the length of life. Then I will add complications.

If the social security mandate results in higher wealth at the early entitlement age, then there is an income effect, tending to lead people who would have retired later than the early entitlement age to retire earlier than they would have otherwise. This income effect is part of an efficient response by the worker to the mandated change in savings (assuming retirement decisions are sensibly made). So we are driven to consider savings behavior as a precondition to examining the effect on retirement decisions. Since savings and labor supply are joint endogenous variables, neither can be fully considered without considering the other (Feldstein, 1974; Munnell, 1974). In this setting, mandating higher savings than the worker would have done without the mandate, together with liquidity constraints that prevent borrowing to offset the mandate, results in higher wealth at the early entitlement age. Because of precautionary savings motives, the savings displacement might not be one-for-one even if a full offset were financially possible.

Empirical estimates of the impact of social security benefits on savings do show an offset, but only a partial offset, far below one-for-one. While some of this is related to precautionary savings, central to this issue is heterogeneity in savings behavior in the population—roughly half of American workers reach retirement age with little discretionary wealth other than from home ownership. Thus, it is plausible that as a result of the mandate many people are able to finance retirement at an earlier age than they could have financed without social security.

Conversely, if there are workers who would have retired before the early entitlement age, then, if the social security mandate is large enough, it will result in more work from them. Indeed, some of these workers may choose to work until the early entitlement age if mandated savings are large enough; that is, if it is not worthwhile to supplement mandated savings in order to finance retirement before the early entitlement age. Thus, while mandating higher savings tends to shorten working lives, limiting access to the benefits financed by mandated savings tends to increase them.

Note that we have identified two reasons for a wave of retirements right at the early entitlement age even if benefits are only age-conditioned, without any requirement of actually retiring. The wave of retirements could be an efficient response to the required savings, including both those who would have retired sooner if not liquidity constrained and those who would have saved less and retired later. Interestingly, while there is a spike in the retirement hazard (probability of retirement conditional on not having retired earlier) at the earliest age of benefit eligibility in the US (Gruber and Wise, 1999), this spike is not present when examining only those with substantial wealth (Kahn, 1988). While this suggests the importance of liquidity constraints, we need also to recognize that the US has an earnings test at age 62, albeit one that increases benefits more than is actuarially fair (breaks even) on average (Diamond and Gruber, 1999).

Normative analysis of these labor supply responses depends on how we think about the savings mandate and how we think about retirement decisions. If we think of workers as being time consistent and with preferences that should be fully respected, then a broad savings mandate loses its main purpose and the restricted access to benefits is a capital market imperfection. With a rational retirement decision as well, then the change in labor supply tends to decrease the harm of an excessive savings mandate. In this setting, the earlier the EEA, the fewer (rational) people harmed by the capital market imperfection. However, if we think of the mandate as offsetting a (possibly time-inconsistent) tendency to save too little for the worker's own good, then a savings mandate can be good and a rational retirement response to a change in savings adds to the good. While not required by logical consistency, it is probably the case that if some savings decisions are not time consistent, some retirement decisions are probably not ideal either. This observation requires recognition of a link between the quality of retirement decisions and the effects of restricted benefit availability. If some people will retire at the EEA when they "ought" to retire later, then an increase in the EEA forces some people to make better decisions.

What is difficult is to find a good empirical basis for estimating the numbers of workers who would be helped and hurt by a change in the EEA.[1] Suggestive evidence of the relevance of

---

[1] There have been studies of data on early retirees trying to estimate how many would find it difficult to adapt to a later EEA (Burkhauser *et al.*, 1996; Kingson and Arsenault, 2000; Leonesio *et al.*, 2000). Due to data limitations, I do not find these studies conclusive.

nonrational retirement for some workers comes from a fall in living standards at retirement of some workers, which is observed in US data (Bernheim *et al.*, 2001), and from the tendency for those living a long time after retirement to have higher poverty rates, although mostly these higher poverty rates are related to widowhood, which raises additional issues of intrafamily redistribution. Inadequate joint-life annuitization contributes to the observed poverty problems and, more generally, a fall in standard of living for widows (Holden and Zick, 1998). The inadequacy of incomes of widows in the US relates to economies of scale in living costs and possible asymmetries in resource use in some couples. There may also be concern about people who retire early and spend their available wealth with an expectation of then accessing benefits for the poor.

One could approach a theory of the optimal EEA as balancing the capital market imperfections for rational early retirees with the potential gain for some nonrational retirees moving to later retirement. On one hand is the efficiency cost of increases in the age because it causes a further delay in retirement for workers who would rationally retire earlier but cannot finance early retirement because of liquidity constraints. On the other hand is the possible gain from forcing continued work for workers who would retire too soon for their own good (or that of their spouses). These two elements, which are central for determining a good early entitlement age, are both hard to measure. Economists tend not to worry about people working too long, either for their own good or to "free up jobs" for others. The latter issue is much more important to the public than to economists who recognize that market responses and adequate macro policy can adjust the availability of jobs, although government regulations and actual macro policy can leave sustained unemployment problems. Nevertheless, since it tends to have effects for a long time, inducing early retirement is an expensive policy compared with others that might be pursued.

Beyond a mandate to save with the same market return as the worker would have had anyway, there are several ways in which a worker could have more or less wealth at early entitlement age because of social security. The present discounted value (PDV) of benefits might differ from the accumulated value of taxes because of transfers—across cohorts and within each cohort. Such transfers will have income effects as well. Across cohorts, redistribution could be done in a lump-sum fashion, although generally it is not so that the marginal return to work is increased for some cohorts and decreased for others. Within cohorts, asymmetric information implies that at least some labor supply decisions must be distorted in order to redistribute, since lump-sum taxes are not feasible. Similarly it is also impossible to provide insurance against bad labor market outcomes without distorting the labor market. One needs to balance the redistribution and insurance gains against the efficiency losses in thinking about policy in this realm.

There are three approaches to benefit redistribution that are widely used. One is a guaranteed minimum pension, second is a supplementary flat benefit for everyone and third is a progressive benefit formula. The three approaches have different patterns of labor market distortions at different earnings levels. The guaranteed minimum has high distortions for a small portion of the earnings distribution, as those below the minimum have zero marginal benefit increase from additional work and some of those above the minimum prefer a drop to the minimum benefit level. In contrast, the other two approaches involve smaller distortions for a larger population. Thus, in general, there appears to be no simple ranking of these from an efficiency point of view. Indeed this question is ripe for the type of optimization analysis that Mirrlees applied to the income tax.[2] These approaches affect both retirement and earlier labor supply decisions and I will return to them below.

Separate from redistribution, the PDV of benefits might differ from the accumulated value of taxes because the rate of return on assets held by social security might differ from the rate of return that the worker would have realized. This difference might be part of better or worse investing (net of administrative costs) by the social security authorities, an issue touched on in the first lecture in terms of the quality of individual and collective investment choices and the economies of scale in investing and so lower administrative costs of centralized investing.

Arguments that a savings mandate is good take two forms (apart from the poor argument that strongly encouraging early

---

[2] Since giving these lectures, I have made a start on this issue in Diamond (forthcoming).

retirement is a sensible way to deal with unemployment among the young). The argument on the right is that for altruistic reasons, taxpayers will provide some level of benefits to the elderly to limit poverty. Anticipating such a transfer would induce some workers not to save in order to benefit from this altruism. Thus, despite reluctance to support government mandates as interferences with liberty, some on the right argue that the mandate is appropriate to prevent free-riding—it is making people pay for what they would receive for free. In contrast, the argument on the left is that many people will not save enough for their own retirement—that people show dynamic inconsistency in their decision-making. Therefore, the government should have some level of mandate in order to protect people from themselves. Moreover, some people forced to save will agree with this—a form of self-paternalism. While there are also insurance market failure arguments, the paternalism argument is central.

Note that the argument on the right is a justification only for a mandate that does not extend above the level of benefits that would be provided by the government (and, possibly, private charity). In contrast, the argument on the left is concerned with replacement rates for workers well up the income distribution, as well as being concerned with poverty. As a philosophical basis for intervention where liberty is highly valued, I find the argument on the right unpersuasive, as I elaborate below. Whether one agrees with that or not, it should be noted that governments, both democratic and non-democratic, have commonly set up systems that have mandates providing benefits to earners that extend well above the poverty line. Thus, consideration of how to design such a system well is necessary for analysts even if they do not agree with the underlying social consensus.

The argument on the right has a structure that seems odd to me. The logic of the argument is that A is driven by altruism to give something to B. Therefore, it is ethically appropriate to mandate that B change behavior (interfering with B's liberty) in order to protect A from A's good intentions. Actual policy cannot distinguish between workers who would save if there were not expected benefits for the elderly and those who would not save either way. That is, redistributing from B to A (relative to no government savings mandate) is argued to be ethically appropriate since there is altruism on the part of A and free riding by some Bs.

That is, it is deemed ethical to compel B to save in order to protect A from A's own altruism. But while some of these Bs may be free riding in the sense that they would save if A were not altruistic, other Bs might not save anyway (rationally or nonrationally) and they are being compelled to save as well. If compelled to save, some of these Bs are harmed, not just net of A's altruism, but also relative to a world without A's altruism. For example, Bs with a short life expectancy may not save because they anticipate dying before retirement age, and so foresee neither a return from forced savings nor a gift from A if there were no forced saving. Such Bs would be harmed by forced savings. If the argument on the right is looking for a Pareto improvement (relative to no compulsion and no altruism) then it cannot be found once we recognize the presence of short-lived nonsavers.

The argument on the left has similar force to arguments for redistribution generally once we recognize that some savings decisions are not based on a consistent lifetime preference structure. Indeed the literature about such behavior often uses the concept of multiple selves in developing a theory of savings behavior that is behaviorally more accurate than a single lifetime optimization. Balancing the mandate's positive and negative impacts on different workers is not a difficulty for a social welfare function approach.[3]

Because I am eager to get into the uncertainty discussion, I do not digress to consider alternative models of savings behavior that involve time inconsistency. (See, e.g. the quasi-hyperbolic discounting models of Laibson (1997) and my use of the approach to consider savings and retirement decisions in ongoing work together with Koszegi (1999).) But this is a fertile area for research.

2.1.2. *Earnings or Retirement Test*

While Chile and Sweden allow all workers above the early entitlement age to claim benefits with no additional conditions, many countries restrict access to benefits to a combination of age and low earnings, at least for some ages. For example, in the US workers between 62 and 65 (or more exactly between the EEA of 62 and the normal retirement age, which is slowly moving from 65 to 67)

---

[3] For the workings of a mandate in such a setting, see von Weizsaecker (2000).

lose $1 of benefits for each $2 dollars of earnings above a limit that is indexed to average wages. Workers above the normal retirement age can claim benefits independent of earnings.[4]

So how does a requirement for low earnings as a condition for benefits affect retirement decisions? And what are the normative consequences of such a requirement? Both of these depend on how benefits adjust when they are claimed after a delay. In this certainty setting, if the PDV of future benefits increases to just offset the lost benefits (and additional payroll taxes on work), then there is no implicit tax on work coming from the earnings test. A defined contribution system where assets earn the market return satisfies this condition. So too, does a DB system with sufficient "actuarial" adjustment to benefits. Indeed in the US, on average 62-year-old workers are subsidized, not taxed, for working an additional year (Diamond and Gruber, 1999). Of course, this means that some workers are subsidized while others are taxed at the margin. However, many European countries do so little adjustment of benefits that implicit taxes are very high (as they were in the US beyond age 65 before the delayed retirement credit was increased and then the earnings test was eliminated beyond the normal retirement age). An obvious lesson is to avoid very high implicit taxes, which can be done with either DB or DC systems despite the presence of an earnings test. However, we need to recognize that some workers will not give adequate weight to larger future benefits when considering retirement.

By paying benefits based solely on age (without an earnings test), or by increasing future benefits to offset the nonpayment of benefits as a consequence of work, a social security system can avoid any implicit tax on continued work past retirement age, at least if everyone has the same life expectancy and discount rate. But is either such approach optimal? There are three reasons to think otherwise, before getting into issues raised by different stochastic life expectancies. One is the provision of insurance for a short career, second is redistribution, and third is errors in retirement decisions.

Implicit in the discussion above, and many formal models of social security, is the use of a deterministic model of earnings

---

[4] And workers above age 70 can no longer delay the start of benefits in order to receive larger ones.

opportunities. But earnings opportunities are stochastic. At older ages, loss of a job often implies a large drop in available wages. Technically similar is a stochastic increase in the disutility of work, provided it occurs in a form that is not covered by disability insurance. Presuming an asymmetry in information between a possible retiree and the benefit providing agency, we have the familiar problem of second-best insurance. Thus, the way to provide insurance against a short earnings career is to tax continued work while subsidizing those who stop work early. A series of papers I have written with Mirrlees (1978, 1986, 2000, forthcoming) show that the optimal retirement plan for an *ex ante* homogeneous population has this character. Thus, in this model it is better to have an earnings test that increases benefits for delayed retirement by less than the amount that is actuarially fair.

This analysis has not been extended to cover the circumstance where people differ in earnings levels as well as stochastic realizations of job opportunities. With an earnings test that allows low earners to work and collect benefits, those not receiving benefits tend to have earnings above the overall average. Thus, there may also be a redistribution basis for an adjustment that is less than actuarially fair in a restrictive setting of a relatively noncomplex benefit formula. That is, it may make sense to put part of the weight of redistribution in the benefit formula and part in the adjustment for delayed claiming of benefits. Even without the stochastic element, those with higher earnings level may also enjoy a profile of available wages at different ages with relatively higher wages later. In a setting of restricted complexity in tax and benefit rules, this pattern seems likely to be a reason for taxation on both length of career and level of earnings, and so taxation on continued work—although I have not seen any work exploring this issue.

Third, we come to the question of the rationality of the retirement decision. It is not implausible that some individuals act as if current benefits are of greater significance than increases in future benefits of the same PDV. Then an actuarially fair earnings test acts like an apparent implicit tax on work. Is it worth having an earnings test anyway? The answer depends on whether the same undervaluing of future benefits will affect the undervaluing of future consumption when making consumption decisions. If so, the division of the population between those who would have continued working anyway and those who will be induced to retire by the earnings test matters for evaluating an earnings test. That is, elimination of the earnings test has two effects. One is to encourage some people to work who would otherwise have retired in order to receive benefits. That is a gain. Second, some of the people who would have worked and not claimed benefits may now work and claim benefits and, as a result, consume more while still working, being left with less when older and retired (or leaving behind a survivor). That may be a loss. Balancing these two effects can be approached by having an earnings test at some ages but not others. Indeed, the recent debate in the US leading up to the legislation that reduced the age at which benefits could be collected without an earnings test was couched in these terms (Gruber and Orszag, 2000).[5]

2.1.3. Mandated Annuitization

In addition to restricting the age at which benefits can be claimed, it is common to restrict the form of benefit receipt. While there may be a choice between phased withdrawals and annuitization and while some lump-sum withdrawal may be allowed, I want to focus on the common (but not universal) mandate to annuitize. This mandate needs to be described in terms of the risk classes that are used to determine benefit levels given accumulation (or benefit levels given past earnings in a DB system). I will proceed by first considering the mandate where life expectancy is uniform and then considering some of the issues that arise from hetero-geneity in perceived life expectancy at different ages.

In order to consider the effects of mandatory annuitization, we need to consider the private annuity market. While some countries have very well-developed and low-cost group annuity markets, individual annuity markets are thin and expensive everywhere. Part of the problem, I believe, is the failure of many people to understand the purpose and benefit associated with annuities. Generally, cognitive psychologists find that people have trouble understanding the properties of stochastic variation. In the case

---

[5] Some favored making benefits available without an earnings test starting at the EEA of 62, as opposed to the legislation which preserved the earnings test between EEA and the normal retirement age, which is slowly rising from 65 to 67.

of annuities, the popularity of years-certain annuities seems to me evidence of successful marketing that would not happen if people had better understanding of the purpose of annuities. For example, a 10-years certain annuity would pay benefits as long as the beneficiary is alive but would also go on paying benefits until 10 years after the annuity has begun in the event that the annuitant dies before that date. The appeal of this is that the total financial return in the case of an early death is larger than it would otherwise be, at a cost of the total financial return being smaller than it would otherwise be in the case of a death beyond the 10-year guarantee. In other words, monthly benefits are reduced if there is also a guaranteed payment period, with the guaranteed payments going to one's heirs. In contrast, without the guarantee, the same level of annuity could be purchased as with the guarantee at a lower cost. Then, the heirs could be given the money saved by not purchasing the guarantee. Thus, purchasing a guarantee converts a safe sum for the heirs into a random bequest—one that is declining with the time until death. Thus, adding a guarantee appears to be purchasing a gamble, not increasing the level of insurance. It does not appear to make good sense. And calling it a guarantee rather than a gamble is framing an increase in risk as a decrease in risk.

The annuitization decision is one where money illusion in the form of preferring nominal to indexed annuities seems particularly widespread, particularly in countries that do not have much experience with price indexing. While there is an adverse selection basis for some people preferring nominal annuities in a low inflation variance environment (since nominal annuities are front loaded relative to real annuities), I do not think that this explains the nature of the equilibrium.

For simplicity, and approximating actual behavior, I will assume that the level of annuity available to a worker varies dollar-for-dollar with the level of annuity provided by social security. That is, I will treat the annuities market that is little used as if it did not exist. It is also the case that a well-run mandatory system can offer annuities with lower administrative costs than is available in the market. Then, a worker who appreciates the value of an annuity will value the retirement benefits financed from taxes more than their actuarial cost. This appreciation yields an extra return to work from the insurance value of receiving a marginally larger annuity (Crawford and Lilien, 1981). On the other hand, the value of annuitization may be underappreciated, which is consistent with a reluctance of individuals to purchase them. Thus the pure insurance value of a larger annuity may not be (fully) appreciated.

Apart from the impact on the labor market, it is appropriate to recognize the impact on expected utility of both the worker and potential heirs. An actuarially fair annuity significantly raises expected utility with the standard formulation of utility (Mitchell *et al.*, 1999). When combined with the possibility of workers who spend more rapidly than is optimal, and so have declining consumption, annuitization (together with a liquidity constraint) has a further advantage of preventing some of the decline in consumption. Further, we can recognize that people get used to a standard of living, so that declining consumption is even more costly than in a model with intertemporally additive preferences. With such intertemporally nonadditive preferences, a lack of annuitization would become even more important (Diamond and Mirrlees, 2000; Davidoff *et al.*, 2001).

Of course, annuitization can lower expected bequests and so affect potential heirs adversely. A worker can prevent this effect by purchasing life insurance. However in the US, there is not much of this that I am aware of, except as a tax avoidance device. And heirs, when they become older, will themselves gain from annuitization, assuming we are considering a long-run program. Thus, annuitization can lower the level of capital in the economy, although this can be readily offset by other government policies such as reducing the national debt.

As a bottom line, in an economy with homogeneous life expectancy, mandated annuitization is a benefit for workers who would not purchase annuities but should and for workers who would annuitize without the mandate (from better terms than offered in the private market). Its impact on the labor market depends on whether workers recognize the advantages of annuitization even though they would not have purchased annuities.

2.1.4. Heterogeneity in Life Expectancy and Risk Classes

The analysis of annuitization becomes particularly interesting when we consider heterogeneity in life expectancy. There is heterogeneity we are aware of *ex ante*, as between men and women, for example, and heterogeneity that develops as people have different health experiences and learn about their underlying potential for longevity. At whatever age one wants to do the calculation, from birth onwards, perceived life expectancy varies in the population. Moreover, even if we try to have multiple-risk classes and to refine annuitization as much as possible, there will remain heterogeneity within each risk class. This heterogeneity affects both lifetime income distribution and labor market incentives.

If there is no earnings test, then mandatory annuitization rules affect separately the return from a year of work and the return from a delay in claiming benefits. With an earnings test, these incentives interact, as we will see.

First, let us examine mandatory annuitization where there is no choice—benefits just start at a given age. Then, with a single-risk class (uniform pricing of annuities), there will be redistribution, on average, across groups. For example, women on average live longer than men. Thus, on average there is redistribution from men to women. It should be noted that for a given age at retirement and given level of wealth to finance retirement, someone with a longer life expectancy is poorer in the sense of less able to finance monthly consumption while alive, so some such redistribution would be part of a utilitarian optimization. It is also worth noting that life expectancy varies among women and among men. Thus, a man and a woman with the same life expectancy would not get the same benefit if there were annuity pricing based only on gender. Thus, a system with two risk classes "redistributes" from a woman with a given life expectancy to a man with the same life expectancy, even though, on average, a single-risk class redistributes from men to women. Similarly, *ceteris paribus*, people with higher education, income, or social status tend to live longer than those with lower levels. Thus, a system with a single-risk class tends to redistribute from poorer groups to richer groups. That is seen in the US as one of the justifications for a progressive benefit formula. Without entering into a discussion of the relative importance of different redistributions, there is the simple point that when risk classes contain heterogeneous risks (as they inevitably will) then any structure of risk classes will involve some redistribution. Making annuitization voluntary does not make this go away, although it changes both the distribution and the efficiency of equilibrium.

A similar issue arises even if the population is identical *ex ante*, but develops information about life expectancy over time (Brugiavini, 1993; Sheshinski, 1999). Because annuitization tends to be done at a single time, the use of a single-risk class provides insurance against reaching retirement and being classified as having a long-life (and so receiving a low annuity benefit). Individuals want to transfer benefits from states where annuity benefits are high to states where they are low. A single-risk class, rather than health-based risk classifications, accomplishes this transfer. Rolling annuitization is another approach. But the labor market incentives depend on risk classification as well. Thus, use of a single-risk class subsidizes the work of those with longer lives, while taxing the work of those with shorter lives. Multiple-risk classes tend to decrease the taxes and subsidies, improving labor market incentives. Thus, there is a tension. Using more risk classes increases risk while tending to get labor market incentives better. In general, one cannot tell which concern is more important.

These issues arise whenever there is mandatory annuitization at a given age. Further issues arise when workers can choose when to annuitize. That is, if workers are eligible to claim benefits but can delay claiming in order to receive a larger benefit thereafter, some workers will choose to do so, as can be seen in the US (Coile *et al.*, forthcoming). If the adjustment is actuarially fair for the entire population, then it will be less than fair for some and more than fair for others. Thus, some workers will claim right away even if they would delay if the system were fair for them individually (in order to get more insurance value from a higher level of annuitization), and the reverse holds for some other workers. Thus, we have a second-best setting, where the design of the annuity adjustment factor is a possible parameter affecting efficiency. Moreover, if annuity pricing is done on a market basis, it is the set of people who do delay claiming who determine the size of the actuarial adjustment.

In this setting, we can consider the merits of allowing choice, given the early entitlement age (although choice of an early entitlement age should be made jointly with whether there is choice on when to start an annuity). The basis of such a consideration would also include concern about the understanding of the benefits of annuitization and possibly excessive discounting of future needs. But these elements are most likely to be a concern for those who do not delay, so analysis of allowing delay is not seriously affected. If delay is allowed on terms that break even (net) for those who do delay, so that pricing is not changed for others, then this is a Pareto gain. Since the long-lived are more likely to delay claiming, this is also a Pareto gain if pricing is done on an actuarial basis for the claimants at each age, since prices improve for those not delaying. Thus, allowing delay of claiming is good in a setting where there is no earnings test.

With mandatory annuitization and no earnings test, the incentive for another year of work depends on life expectancy since some of the return to that work comes in the form of an annuity priced at the mandated price. Thus, there is a tax on some workers and a subsidy on other workers for an additional year of work. The effects on retirement and on claiming interact if there is a retirement test, and so there is a need to retire in order to claim benefits. Conversely, there may be no need to claim just because one has stopped work. In this case, the loss from delayed claiming for those with short life expectancies is an added burden on work. However, the gain from delayed claiming for those with long life expectancies is not an extra subsidy for work for those who are not liquidity constrained since that delay is possible whether the worker retires or not.

In practice, I suspect that this issue is far less important than the fact that many countries have systems with such low returns to delayed claiming that there is a large tax on work on everyone. Fixing such systems is high on the agenda of needed reforms in some countries.

With a DB system, one can increase benefits for a delayed start in a way that is actuarially fair on average or choose to encourage or discourage work relative to this standard. To evaluate a system with this mix of incentives for different people (and with no other issues) would be similar to the standard second-best problem that arises from the use of uniform pricing when costs are not uniform across purchasers (Diamond and Rothschild, 1989: chapter 14). A DC system with mandatory annuitization faces the same diversity in individual incentives. And without mandatory annuitization, we have similar issues coming from voluntary annuitization.

Thus, limited information and annuitization affect both lifetime income distribution and retirement incentives. The same point carries over to labor supply at younger ages.

So the bottom line here is that mandatory or voluntary annuitization inevitably includes a distortion of the retirement decision—some people are being implicitly taxed and some are being implicitly subsidized as they perceive different life expectancies, and so different lengths of time for receiving benefits. The alternative of abandoning annuitization for either lump-sum transfers or phased withdrawals lowers the value of the return to work by giving up the insurance value of annnuitization. In this setting, markets are incomplete, with the incompleteness functioning somewhat like a distorting tax. The entire picture is made more complex because we do not know how people perceive the value of an annuity relative to actuarial calculations when making retirement decisions. Nor do we know how well people can judge their own life expectancies (although there is evidence showing some understanding in the Health and Retirement Survey: Hurd *et al.*, 1999).

2.1.5. *Treatment of the Family and Joint-life Annuitization*

It is common to require some protection for other members of the family in mandatory annuitization programs. (Mandating life insurance to protect children is another facet of social security programs.) Indeed there is a long history of some government involvement in the protection of members of the family. For example, there are restrictions in the US and Sweden on the ability to leave one's spouse with too small a percentage of one's estate. It needs to be recognized that some form of joint-life annuitization—continuation of some benefits for a surviving spouse, may well be different from what a worker would choose. Indeed the evidence in the US is that workers tended strongly to single life annuities in pension programs that allowed choice before government rules led to significant changes. Insofar as a worker is not giving adequate attention to the worker's spouse, a mandate requiring such benefits may affect labor market decisions in a way that works similarly to a labor market implicit tax distortion.

Analysis of joint-life annuitization raises similar issues as does treatment of the family by the annual income taxation. There are three tax principles one might want to espouse. One is progressive marginal income taxation. A second is that the taxation of an individual not vary with whether that individual is married or not. And a third is that two couples should be taxed the same if they have the same total income. As is well known, these three principles are mutually inconsistent. One cannot have equal treatment of individuals and equal treatment of couples without having linearity of taxation. So one needs to choose among the principles or to compromise them. If some couples do in fact share their incomes, then, it is fair to treat different couples in the same final (after-sharing) positions with the same tax treatment. But some couples do not share and individual decisions on marriage are affected by tax consequences. Thus, personally, I am a compromiser, since I see real merit in all three, but there are other views.

Mandatory joint-life annuitization (in some fraction) is one way of intervening within the family to require a pattern of benefit flows that vary between the times when both members of a couple are alive and when only one is. Assuming, again, that people will not make such arrangements for themselves, or undo such arrangements through other transactions, then such an intervention needs to be judged on its outcomes. In the US, the poverty rates of elderly widows is much higher than the poverty rates of elderly couples—by a factor of three or more (there is some ambiguity in how to measure poverty relatively for single people and couples). Moreover, studies following women into widowhood find a sharp drop in resources relative to needs (Holden and Zick, 1998). An alternative to mandatory joint-life annuitization is mandatory annual sharing of earnings for earnings records or account deposits. Either form of mandate raises concern about the age of access to benefits. Access to only a fraction of benefits based on a single earnings record may inhibit retirement (because earnings records have been shared). On the other hand, later access can finance higher benefits, which may be relevant not just for the worker but also for a surviving spouse. Also complicating the story is that husbands and wives are typically of different ages, so the timing of access to retirement benefits becomes complicated with some methods of resolving this tension. In the US, there is serious discussion of increasing the benefits for survivors at the expense of benefits for couples (Burkhauser and Smeeding, 1994). While policy changes to help widows have been much discussed for many years in the US, there has been little basic research on this issue.

There is also the question of whether joint-life annuity rules should be done with or without cross-subsidization.[6] That is, in any progressive system that recognizes families, there is a need to calibrate a couple against an individual relative to the standard for determining the direction of redistribution. And since redistribution affects labor supply, analysis is made more complicated when two workers are affected by interacting rules.

These issues are made more complicated by considerations that reflect entire lifetimes, while people may be married for only parts of them, and some will divorce and remarry. There is no simple set of rules for handling divorce that will be fully satisfactory across the very diverse settings of different couples. Since it is not just earnings during the period of marriage, but also changes in human capital, and so later earnings, that are affected by labor market behavior during a period of marriage, the issue is complex. While divorce settlements outside social security can take into account the effects within social security, they are not a perfect substitute. As far as I know, these issues have not had much academic study, although governments must make rules to deal with these varying situations.

2.2. Labor Supplies at Younger Ages

The issues that affect the retirement decision are present when younger workers are considering their labor supply. In addition, there are issues arising from the long lag between the earnings of a young worker and the eventual possible receipt of retirement benefits.

2.2.1. *Mandated Savings*

Insofar as people are being forced to save more than they would choose to and insofar as additional covered earnings add to the

---

[6] In Chile, the mandate for joint-life protection out of the DC accumulation has no cross-subsidization. In the US, the provision of spouse and survivor benefits redistributes from single workers to couples and among couples with different earnings. While one might want some cross-subsidization, the US pattern could be improved.

amount they are forced to save, forced savings may affect labor decisions in a way that parallels a standard tax distortion. If forced savings are earning a market rate, 7 percent, say, but people are evaluating this consequence of covered work by discounting future benefits at 18 percent, say, then the current perceived value of future benefits is far less than the current taxes paid. For example, $1 compounded at 7 percent for 20 years and then discounted at 18 percent is only worth $0.14. Changes in benefit rules are then of less consequence than they would be without this high discounting. That is, if young people are not paying much attention to retirement issues, then the payroll tax may be mostly viewed as a tax of a similar value however benefits are designed. This effect shows up both in labor supply and in the choice between covered and non-covered work, which, in many countries, coincides with the distinction between the formal and informal sectors. And it shows up in tax evasion.

It is important to recognize that, as with a payroll tax not linked to benefits, the supply of labor from rational workers may go up or down as a consequence of a savings mandate that exceeds what the worker would choose. In the pure tax case, we have an income effect—less lifetime income implies lower consumption, implying a higher marginal utility of consumption and so a greater utility value of marginal work. But marginal work returns less net of tax than gross of tax. The product of these two effects, one raising and the other lowering the marginal consumption utility from additional work is theoretically indeterminate. Similarly, a high mandated savings will increase the current marginal utility of consumption while lowering a future marginal utility of consumption. Additional work increases consumption at both times, which is worth less than if the additional earnings could all be consumed at the time of highest marginal utility of consumption. However, since one marginal utility has risen and the other has fallen, and we cannot say in general which change is larger, the weighted average of marginal utilities may go up or down, and so the marginal value of additional earnings may go up or down.

While some have argued that changing to individual DC accounts would have a large effect on labor market efficiency among young workers, these arguments suggest that any effect will be small. Empirical experience is supportive of this view.

Writing about Argentina, Rofman (2000) finds that "The stagnation in the number of contributors to the SIJP is worrisome, since it was expected that the introduction of the individual account scheme and the reductions in employers' contributions established in recent years would act as incentives to increase participation." (p. 19) Schmidt-Hebbel (1999) does find less growth in informal work in Chile than in other Latin American countries and attributes this to pension reform. Even if this attribution is correct, it needs to be noted that the Chilean reform lowered the payroll tax rate as well as changing from DB to DC. Thus we cannot separate the effect of lower taxes *per se* from the effect of a change in the form of benefits.

Note that the quality of design of a DC system matters for the labor market effect—the greater the administrative costs the lower the return to work. As noted in Lecture 1, the cost of administering DC social security systems varies greatly with system design.

Another issue that arises is the perceptions of workers. With DC, workers have trouble knowing how much they will have in retirement in annual consumption. Thus, they may have trouble evaluating mandated savings in terms of marginal utilities. There are suggestions that workers overestimate the retirement consumption that can be financed from a given lump sum, but it is difficult to evaluate this possibility. On the other hand, with DB, it is complex to know how much a possibly more predictable level of benefits will be changed by additional work. So it is unclear how workers evaluate labor market incentives. I suspect that in DB systems, workers overvalue earnings at some times and undervalue them at others. It does not make for a tidy picture or an easy problem to estimate empirically.

Many workers will not survive until retirement age. While the presence of dependents is a basis for life insurance for such early deaths, some workers will have no dependents and for others there remains the issue of the possibly differential value of resources conditional on survival to retirement age rather than the value of bequests should there be an earlier death. A defined benefit system gives larger benefits to those reaching retirement age, financed by the estates of those who do not reach retirement age. The NDC system here does this explicitly, redistributing the accounts of those who die in proportion to accounts of survivors in the same age cohort. For someone who does not value bequests at all, the accumulation in a mandatory savings DC account with bequest rights is of no value if he or she dies before reaching retirement age. Thus, a defined contribution system involves distorting taxation of those with lesser interest in bequests because of the failure to convert the value of their estates should they die before retirement into consumption if they survive, which is of greater value to them. I note in passing that the expected number of deaths before retirement age is significant. Using US life tables, roughly 15 percent of 21-year-old workers will not survive until retirement age, with more men than women dying early, of course.

2.2.2. Comparing DB and DC Systems

In a DC system, the weighting of earnings at different ages in determining benefits is done by compounding contributions at the rate of return. A DB system generally weights different years somewhat differently in two ways—one is compounding that occurs through the method of indexing, and the second is using earnings in only some years. Some DB systems count earnings in a fixed number of years, ignoring earnings in other years completely. For example, in the US, retirement benefits are based on the thirty-five best (wage-indexed) earnings years.[7] In a system like this, the labor market incentives depend critically on the number of years included in calculating an average wage for benefit purposes. (There is also the distinction as to whether it is the best years or the last years of earnings that are used.) For a social security system like that in the US, with a 35-year averaging period, the combination of the relevance of early earnings for possible disability benefits and the uncertainty as to which years will be among the best thirty-five do still give significant labor market incentives for young full-time workers. The NDC approach uses all years. A more complex system could have differing weights on years with different earnings.

Another approach uses a very short number of years and gives some weight to early years by multiplying average earnings over

---

[7] Early years, but not late ones, are indexed. This is an oddity in the law that should be fixed.

a short period by a count of a number of years with earnings above some minimum. This was the system here in Sweden before the reform. With this approach, labor market incentives will be poor—with very low incentives in years where earnings levels will not count for benefits and a strong incentive to manipulate the system and possibly work greatly to excess in years that do count. For example, the pension system for subway workers in Boston has workers within three years of retirement working vast quantities of overtime in order to enhance their retirement benefits. This has led to crashes from workers asleep at the controls. Some communist countries based benefits on the last year of earnings—a system clearly not viable in a market economy. What is a challenge in that case is to design a transition to a good system—a transition that may need to be made slowly because of a lack of earnings records. It is better to recognize that an explicit transition is needed rather than designing a long-run system and merely adapting it to data availability.

Among DB systems with long averaging periods, there has been some, but not much work on the design of an optimal system. There are two issues here—one is providing some insurance against a small number of very low earnings years. Evaluating the insurance aspects of system design is sensitive to the stochastic structure of earnings (Dulitzky, 1998).[8] Second is consideration of the desired level of retirement income as relating to a standard of living to which new retirees have become accustomed—a standard that is likely to depend more on earnings in later years of life than those in a worker's twenties and thirties. However, given a positive correlation between higher earnings levels and steeper earnings trajectories, one needs to be careful about the progressivity in the benefit formula along with the length of the averaging period being used. Just as differential life expectancies by income level are a reason for a progressive benefit formula, so

[8] In early years, workers do not know whether the current year will count as part of the N years that will enter the benefit formula. Thus, rather than perceiving a zero marginal benefit, there is a positive expected marginal benefit. Conversely, in the stochastic realizations of earnings when there is low wages in some later years, there is a zero in marginal benefits in the later years. A second effect happens within any year. Early in the year a worker does not know what earnings will be over the entire year. Thus, there is a possibility early in the year that this particular year will not be part of the highest N years, a possibility that largely gets resolved in the course of the year.

too heavier weight on later years of earnings are a reason for a progressive benefit formula.

For a system that uses close to a full career earnings record, we have real similarity between DC and DB systems. With a DC system taxes on earnings in different years are compounded by a rate of return. With a DB system, earnings in different years are compounded by some index, for example, an index of average wages in the US and Sweden. If wage growth and interest rates are similar, the outcomes are similar. Generally we would expect that interest rates are somewhat higher than wage growth rates. In this case, the DB system gives a smaller net tax for work later in life, while the DC system gives a smaller net tax for work earlier in life (zero), when comparing two systems with the same tax rate and budget balance. If there were no other sources of distortions, the DC system would be more efficient than the DB system (ignoring the provision of insurance). But there is no simple dominance of one over the other in the presence of other labor market distortions. Indeed, with a progressive annual income tax and age-earnings profiles that are generally increasing in real terms, the marginal income tax rate is rising with age, on average. Thus, a well-designed DB system may well have better labor market outcomes since the overall tax burden, income tax plus net tax from social security, will vary less over the life-cycle. That is, income taxes are lower on the young and net social security taxes are higher. Therefore, without a detailed calculation, one cannot reach an efficiency conclusion. In any case the difference is likely to be much smaller than the difference between DB systems with long and short averaging periods.

2.2.3. *Types of Redistribution*

With either type of system there is a choice as to the design of the redistribution institution. For example, Chile has a guaranteed minimum pension for everyone with sufficient years of coverage within social security. (There is also a minimum income for all the elderly, one that includes an asset test and is at only half the level of the minimum pension.) In contrast, Argentina provides a flat benefit for everyone with enough coverage. And Sweden is going from providing a uniform benefit to providing a minimum guarantee with a gradual phase out, so that the range subject to full implicit taxation of benefits is restricted and followed by a range where the implicit tax rate is lower, but covers a wider band of pension levels.[9]

Providing a minimum pension costs the treasury less than providing the same level of benefit to everyone. But that is not the measure we are really interested in. One needs to look at implicit taxes as well as explicit taxes. With a flat benefit for everyone, the taxes that finance the benefit are the taxes distorting the labor market. With a minimum benefit, in addition to the taxes that finance the benefit, there is the zero marginal benefit for earnings until the minimum benefit level is reached. This lack of marginal benefit represents an implicit tax that also affects labor market behavior. While analysis of optimal income taxes has not been extended to pension systems, it is plausible that many of the results will carry over. If so, the implicit taxes in a guaranteed minimum benefit system are not likely to be optimal. That is a high tax and a discrete jump to a much lower tax is not likely to be optimal. Plausibly, the Argentinian system with a flat benefit is not optimal either, since somewhat higher implicit taxes on low earners has the advantage of lowering benefits for many workers at higher earnings levels. (My own recent research (1998) has called for a U-shape pattern of marginal income tax rates, as is in fact common in income tax systems. Whether this would extend to social security needs analysis.) The US system does have a smooth pattern of redistribution with earnings level, a style that can be built into either DB or DC systems. The Argentinian and Chilean systems do have the advantage of simplicity.

Evaluations of efficiency need to compare entire systems, not just portions of systems.[10] Moreover, it needs to be recognized that there are no other regularly used tools which do redistribution

---

[9] The guarantee does not relate to the actual DC pension, just a blowup of NDC.

[10] In considering income distribution, one needs to consider the interaction of the social security system with the income tax system. A good way to integrate is that followed in Chile and here in Sweden—mandated contributions are tax deductible and all benefits are taxed, with no taxes on accumulation. In contrast, Australia has partial taxation (relative to the rest of the tax system) at all three stages—contribution, accumulation, and benefit payments. This leads to a complex system, made more complex by changes in tax rates over time together with grandfathering earlier contributions. Moreover, the complexity makes it difficult to design good policies.

based on such long-term earnings histories. That is, a tax-transfer system based on annual incomes cannot replicate a system based on lifetime considerations. There is an important distinction between the temporarily poor and the lifetime poor. Also, a redistribution system based on pension benefits (i.e. past earnings), and not total current income, has the advantage of not being an implicit tax on savings to nearly the same extent (there is a small interaction since marginal income tax rates vary with total taxable income). This effect on savings is an important reason to maintain an earnings-related system and not have just an annual income-related system.

There are two ways to build redistribution into a DC system. One is based on the actual lifetime accumulation (or a virtual accumulation, accumulated mandated savings at a hypothetical interest rate—a relevant alternative to lower distortions on portfolio choice). The other is based on annual earnings. (See, e.g. Boskin *et al.*, 1988.) With a lifetime basis for redistribution, the effects are similar to those in a progressive DB system. Assuming that the redistribution is on a break-even basis within a cohort, there is subsidization of low lifetime earners and taxation of high lifetime earners. A DC system with nonlinear annual redistribution within a cohort is less efficient from a labor market perspective since some individuals will be taxed in some years and subsidized in others, accomplishing redistribution less efficiently than through a lifetime-based mechanism.

The use of annual redistribution that is not cohort specific would be different since it will tend to subsidize young workers and tax older workers relative to a system that redistributes on a lifetime basis. With no other distortions, such taxation, if nonlinear, would be an increase in distortions. With a progressive income tax, we have some of the effects above, exacerbating the distortions from the progressivity in the income tax rather than relieving them. Even if the system is cohort specific, there will be taxation in some years and subsidization in others for many workers.

2.3. Concluding Remarks

The focus of this chapter has been the direct impacts on labor supplies, without recognizing a role for firms. In countries with relatively small public retirement systems, like the Netherlands and the US, privately-provided, regulated, tax-favored pension systems are likely to fill some of the gap between retirement needs and public provision. Such a mixed system is likely to be more heterogeneous than a uniform national system.[11] Decentralized heterogeneity can have its plusses and minuses and would be a fit subject for study.

[11] I have not discussed the common pattern of public systems that vary by industry or labor type (e.g. blue or white collar) and have historically reflected political power too much rather than sensible design.

Chapter 3   Social Security and the Capital Market

In considering the impact of social security on the capital market, I address two issues. First, I briefly discuss social security and the aggregate capital stock. The similarity between changes in the funding of social security and changes in the level of outstanding public debt makes this familiar territory. Then I discuss social security and the allocation of risk. My context will be an advanced economy, like Sweden or the US, so I will not discuss the role of social security reform in the development of the capital market, as has happened in Chile (see, e.g. Diamond and Valdés-Prieto, 1993).

The topic stands out for two reasons, besides its inherent importance. One is the recognition of some nonrational behavior. Second is the central role played by incomplete markets, arising particularly, but not completely, from the overlapping generations (OLG) structure of the economy.

3.1. Aggregate Capital Stock

The history of social security has had an effect on the current capital stock. While some have tried to quantify this effect using time series econometrics, I think I am in the vast majority in thinking that such regressions are unable to provide a reliable answer. So I will discuss the theoretical framework for approaching the question as a matter of general equilibrium. This approach will also cast light on the normative implications of whatever quantitative results have occurred. Throughout the chapter, I will only consider equilibria where the interest rate is above the growth rate so that there is not dynamic inefficiency from an excess of capital.

I begin with the implications of marginally increasing funding in a given social security system. While I discuss these implications in terms of increasing the funding of an unfunded defined benefit (DB) system, similar analysis holds for replacing part of a DB system with a funded defined contribution (DC) system.

3.1.1. Increased Funding

A defined benefit system has an infinite horizon present discounted value (PDV) budget constraint, including payroll taxes received, possible transfer from general revenues, returns on whatever assets it happens to hold, benefits to be paid and administrative costs that are charged against the system. Since the future is stochastic (and markets are not complete), there is no way of knowing the exact shape of the constraint. Rather, a DB system functions with a constraint on cash flow—being unable to print money and constrained not to borrow, it can only pay benefits to the extent that it has resources, through revenue flows and assets, and transfers received from general revenues. Since a well-run system should not make dramatic changes in either taxes or benefits that come into effect shortly thereafter, such systems try to project likely financial position well into the future, although in different countries such projections are made with varying horizons and varying degrees of independence from politics.

Given any projection, a country can decide to increase the funding of the system. Increased funding can make the system more secure, allow increased future benefits, allow decreased future taxes, and increase national savings (and so the ability to provide the real resources that lie behind the anticipated cash benefits). In some countries benefits are being legislated annually, or even more often. This is not how such a system should work. Other countries pass social security legislation infrequently, adjusting the system to evolving circumstances and maintaining an ability to stay out of short-run crises, at least most of the time. In such a system, the government can decide to increase the funding (on a sustained basis) of the DB system.

Assume that a system proposes to increase funding in the near term. Increased funding can be done in five ways—increase the payroll tax (or other earmarked revenue sources), cut benefits, receive a larger transfer from general revenues, earn more on assets, or cut administrative expenses.[1] While administrative

---

[1] I ignore changes in the extent of coverage.

expenses are extraordinarily high in some less-developed countries, advanced countries tend to have very low administrative costs, so this is not a potential source of significant revenue. Moreover, some countries may spend too little on administrative expenses and so provide too low a level of services. Later, I consider portfolio choice for whatever assets happen to exist. So, now I concentrate on the three remaining options.

Adding to the resources of the system in the near term by increasing its assets changes the PDV budget constraint. Of course, the government could simply reverse itself in the future and take all the resources back, but I want to concentrate on political settings where there is considerable government stability and respect for a fiscally separate social security system. An increase in social security resources is referred to as narrow funding or apparent funding in some writings. It represents an increase in the likelihood of being able to pay given benefits in the future or an ability to pay increased benefits. A central question is what happens to the national capital stock (referred to as broad funding or ultimate funding in these same writings). Using OLG models, we can trace out the various routes by which a change in narrow funding can affect the equilibrium level of national capital. Individuals may react to changes in taxes and benefits (both current and future) by changing their personal savings. The government can respond to the changed fiscal position of social security and the changed position of the rest of the budget by altering its contribution to national savings. The net effect of these responses can change interest rates and wages, which, in turn, feed back on both national savings and the financial position of social security. There are models spelling this out in detail, containing the familiar OLG elements (see, e.g. Diamond, 1997).

In the US debate, some people appear not to understand the central role of the PDV budget constraint. Thus, some people seem to think that transferring resources from a central DB fund to individual DC accounts directly changes national savings. A similar lack of a direct impact on national savings comes if government debt is used to finance individual accounts (thereby making implicit debt explicit). This is wrong, as has been well pointed out in the literature (Geanakoplos *et al.*, 1998; Murphy and Welch, 1998; Sinn, 1999; Diamond, 1999*a*). Thus, it is necessary to repeat the central element—to have a serious impact on national savings through funding, one must raise taxes or cut benefits, or transfer resources from general revenues that would otherwise have been used for consumption, not investment.

As to indirect impacts, individuals might change private savings. If payroll taxes are increased, much of the added revenue will come out of current consumption, not current savings, even if the tax increase is intended for additional benefits. If current benefits are cut, much of the resources freed up will come out of consumption, especially if an increase in future benefits is part of the package. Also, private savings might respond to changes in the confidence that workers have about the future ability of the system to provide benefits. Since consumption depends on expected legislation, and not just current legislation, it is not easy to disentangle the effect of any particular legislation.

Governments might also change the savings on the non-social security budget.[2] An increased transfer from the rest of the budget may change taxes and expenditures, although the exact pattern is unclear. Similarly, improved financing of social security that does not come from the rest of the budget can have political implications. In the US, it is sometimes argued that since Social Security ran a surplus while the rest of the budget had a large deficit from the mid-1980s until recently, those social security surpluses financed the government deficit rather than adding to national savings. Correct analysis is more complex, needing to examine a political counterfactual. US budget deficits were a large problem during this period. If the 1983 legislation had not put Social Security into a surplus position, the deficit in the integrated (or unified) budget would have been larger. The counterfactual to examine is whether in the absence of Social Security surpluses a larger measured deficit would have resulted in tax changes and/or spending changes that would have resulted in more national savings.[3] I am very skeptical. My reading of the politics of the time is that the political difficulties of increasing taxes and of cutting expenditures drove the size of the deficit, not vice versa. Moderate changes in the overall deficit then may have

[2] For analysis of how government budget patterns affect the link between social security and national savings, see Elmendorf and Liebman (2000).

[3] Another potential contribution to national savings comes from the likelihood that the government would have had to pay a higher interest rate on debt issued.

had no effect whatsoever on other budget actions. If this is the correct counterfactual, then all of the social security surplus was saved (at least within the government). Whatever the correct counterfactual, it is clear that analysis of political equilibrium is needed for analysis of the relationship between the fiscal statuses of social security and the rest of the government.[4]

3.1.2. Start-up of a PAYG System

Worldwide, public DB systems have ended up with very little in assets compared with the liabilities implicit in a continuation of the current law governing benefits. While all the feedback effects mentioned above affect the size of the impact, it is plausible that there is a large effect on national capital, even if we cannot measure it with any confidence from time series regressions. While this is now history and cannot be undone (except somewhat through cutting future benefits), we can still examine the effects of having done this. Here, my main message is to step behind the impact on capital to consider the impact on welfare. A decision not to pursue full funding (given actuarial projections) is a decision to have higher benefits or lower taxes in the early days of such a system (or both). Ignoring the feedback effects, we can think of this simply as a tax-transfer plan. Also we can think whether it was good or bad by judging the patterns of redistributions. In the US there was the large plus that considerable benefits were given to poor cohorts, greatly alleviating poverty and saving the federal government revenues in its poverty alleviation programs. On the negative, the distribution of these transfers among members of the early cohorts went disproportionately to the well-off in those cohorts. I suspect this was true in many countries. Let me explain the mechanism at work.

The US, in the 1930s, and Canada, in the 1960s, set up defined benefit systems. Eventually, their benefit formulas were designed

---

[4] The recent brief period when US politicians talked of balancing the budget excluding Social Security (and disagreed on whether to also exclude Medicare) is plausibly one where the surpluses were saved. Now that deficits have returned (as this lecture is being revised at the start of 2002) and newspapers have returned to reporting unified budget deficits (not separating out Social Security), it is still not clear that differences in the levels so reported can drive legislation on taxes and spending.

to use average earnings over nearly a full career. This approach to a DB system is widely seen to be the right approach, since the use of a short averaging period for determining benefits is both highly distorting of the labor market and easy to manipulate. This can result in an excess of undesirable income redistributions and also possibly public disdain. But this design for when the system is mature leaves open the question of how the system should function when workers have fewer years under the system than the averaging period that will eventually be used to determine benefits. In both the US and Canada the answer was simply to use a short (but growing) averaging period until the system became mature. There are two consequences of this approach. One is large redistribution to retirees when the system is immature. This follows from using the same benefit formula across cohorts who had very different numbers of years of paying taxes. The second is that this redistribution goes particularly to high earners not low earners, since benefits (which exceed taxes), and so net transfers, are related to earnings. While the first consequence might be an appropriate response to the low incomes of retirees when the system is immature, the second consequence seems to me to be bad policy. In both the US and Canada, these effects were compounded by also starting with a low tax rate, which was steadily increased over time.

The purpose of giving larger benefits to retirees in the early days was for them to have higher consumption. I pass over Keynesian issues that definitely mattered in the late 1930s. Apart from that, if retirees have higher consumption then it is not surprising that national savings goes down. Indeed the policy would have failed in its intent if this did not happen. So a historic effect of lowering capital is a necessary part of successfully carrying out such a policy and not a basis for complaint, unless the transfers were themselves poor policy. And now we need to ask the same question— do we want to transfer more or fewer resources to future cohorts?

3.2. Risk-sharing

The one fact about the future that is fully predictable is that outcomes will remain unpredictable. This is true for future earnings at both the individual and aggregate levels and for future rates of return on both individual assets and aggregate capital. It is also true for demographic variables—fertility, mortality, net migration. As a consequence, the future finances of social security and its ability to achieve target replacement rates are also uncertain. Adapting to this uncertainty involves two elements. One is the legislated rules controlling social security, which allocate some of these risks to different individuals. Second is the ongoing possibility of new legislation. Indeed, we can think of a social security system as analogous to an incomplete contract (Diamond, 1996). It is to be expected that the future of the system will be revisited by legislators, with current legislation affecting future legislation. The link between current legislation and future outcomes naturally differs across countries, although there are probably some tendencies that hold widely.

There are four aspects of risk sharing that I consider in varying detail. One is the risk inherent in annuities, second is the risky rate of return on assets, third is the risk to cohort-wide earnings, and fourth is risk from the political process. I will not consider risks associated with fertility, which have been explored in the literature (see, e.g. Bohn, 2001; Hassler and Lindbeck, 1997). Risks can be shared among current workers, with current retirees, and with future cohorts. One complication that will be ignored is the role of the government in already spreading some of these risks, particularly through the tax system and the adjustment of public debt. An integrated treatment of taxes and social security is more complex than I address. The focus is on cohort-wide risks, not individual risks.

3.2.1. *Annuitization*

Let me start with annuities. At the time of annuity purchase (or the legislated determination of annual benefit levels), there are several choices that affect risk sharing (risk in the accumulation process is discussed in the next subsection). First, an annuity can be in nominal terms. Despite the risk inherent in unknown future inflation rates, nominal annuities are extraordinarily popular (relative to other annuities). This fits with the level of money illusion that is rampant in populations, particularly those with little ongoing experience with indexation (Shafir *et al.*, 1997). Since annuities are providing benefits for a long time, uncertainty about future price levels gets very large by the time we are considering 80- and 90-year-old survivors. I think economists would generally agree that nominal annuities make little sense.

I consider three alternatives. One is a real annuity, second is a variable annuity based on rates of return, and third is a variable annuity based, at least in part, on earnings growth in the economy. I do not consider annuities, such as those provided by TIAA-CREF which place cohort-wide mortality risks on beneficiaries (Valdés-Prieto, 1998). There is considerable uncertainty and debate about the future evolution of mortality improvement. So, allocating this risk is a significant issue. If done through private insurance companies, we would expect a sizable risk premium. If done through government, then we have similar issues in risk allocation as with other ways in which revenues less expenditures can diverge from projections. There does not appear to be a simple way for the typical worker to hedge cohort mortality risk. For example, a significant medical breakthrough could lower annuity benefits significantly with little notice.[5]

A real annuity shifts the risk in the funding of the annuity to other parties.[6] So one question is whether retirees should bear any of this risk. Optimal risk sharing considerations suggest that some of the risk should be borne by the elderly. But the elderly are generally more risk averse than younger populations who can adjust earnings and are more flexible in their ability to adapt to changes in consumption levels. A counterargument is that those of the elderly who will be leaving significant estates can shift the risk to their heirs, and they can also adapt by holding a less risky portfolio outside social security. Given the risk aversion of the elderly, particularly those with few financial assets, a real annuity does not seem to be a bad choice, but sharing some risk with the elderly may be better if done well. This raises the question of

[5] Holding stocks in companies doing medical research is not an option for workers without significant financial assets. And significant medical breakthroughs are not necessarily highly profitable for previously identifiable companies. Moreover, profitability is likely to depend on how the government regulates or controls the market in medical care.

[6] I do not explore the issue of defining a price index that is optimal for adjusting benefits for a population of retirees. There are good political reasons for use of a widely available price index that is used of all government indexation. Nevertheless, it would be interesting to explore the construction of a price index as a social welfare function optimization.

which risks to shift to the elderly and how much risk. It also leaves the question of whether the risks from offering real annuities should be distributed through the market (e.g. by competitive bidding by insurance companies for group annuities) or through a government institution.[7]

In considering funded annuities, one risk behind the annuities is rate-of-return risk. Thus a variable annuity, where the annuity size adjusts to realized asset returns is an option. But using a fully variable annuity invested in the market portfolio shifts none of this risk to the market. It seems unlikely that that much risk on the elderly is optimal. So some adjustment is called for, perhaps by inclusion of a sizable share of real bonds. Similarly, in a PAYG system with earmarked financing, financial risk is inherent in the uncertainty of the cash flow to the system (which should be adjusted by the future obligations generated by the cash flow). Sweden has kept this risk on retirees, with use of an annuity that is fully adjusted to wage growth. An alternative approach that seems to me more attractive would be an index that is a mix of price and wage indexing—recognizing that that leaves more risk elsewhere in social security. That is, there may have been excessive attention to the financing of risks at the expense of risk sharing in the Swedish reform.

Of course, the right way to think about risk sharing is not by considering social security in isolation, but by considering all of risk sharing through all of the risk allocation mechanisms in the economy. This requires examining what other income sources the elderly have. I do not pursue this issue, implicitly concentrating on the risks borne by people who have little in other incomes (other than health insurance and poverty protection).

By waiting to annuitize until a cohort reaches age 65, the risks are spread differently than if annuity commitments were made on a rolling basis.[8] Let us consider the process. At a single time, interest rates, and then current estimates of future cohort mortality are combined to convert an accumulation (real or notional) into an annuity. Thus, annuitization at retirement means that both interest rate risk and information that is revealed about future

---

[7] I do not consider risk shifting by trade in indices, as discussed by Shiller (1993).

[8] Individual risk classification given cohort mortality was discussed in Lecture 2.

mortality were not insured earlier in time. This timing is easiest to think about in a market setting. Buying annuities from an insurance company on a rolling basis (assuming a single-risk class) involves shifting risks according to expectations at the time of contracting. Since interest rates fluctuate up and down, spreading the interest rate risk seems worthwhile. The issue of who shares mortality risk is complex because of the correlations between mortality improvements in different cohorts. If my cohort is suddenly expected to live longer, so too are likely to be younger and slightly older cohorts who are among the candidates for sharing this risk.

A worker who did not annuitize on a rolling basis could hedge some of the risk in annuity pricing by shifting his or her asset portfolio in the direction of the portfolio used by insurance companies (or the government) to price annuities. In a DB, workers who are not doing significant saving outside social security do not have a portfolio to adjust—and short transactions are limited.

As workers learn about the replacement rates they will receive, they can change their savings rates. They are likely to be aware of variations in rates of return during accumulation, but not in projections of mortality rates nor in the connection between future interest rates and future annuity levels. Regular statements on anticipated benefits might help, but these would be politically difficult to distribute when they report declines in anticipated benefits. How large this risk is depends on how benefits are determined. While DC systems have large rate-of-return risks, a worker in an NDC system needs to reflect on the lower variation in wage growth rates. A DB system will have risks that depend on how the political process adapts—preferably in small steps with advance warning, possibly with large jumps with short warning. As a result of these risks from both accumulation and annuitization processes, members of nearby cohorts can have very different replacement rates, which may generate political pressures. Uncertainty in earnings and a plausibly nonadditive preference structure add to the risk aversion surrounding replacement rates.[9]

---

[9] On the choice of an averaging period to reduce earnings risk, see Dulitzky (1998). On nonadditive preferences and social security optimization, see Diamond and Mirrlees (2000).

3.2.2. Rate-of-Return Risk

Insofar as a social security system has any assets, there is a portfolio choice. Most systems have held government debt. Increasingly, there is a move to holding a diversified portfolio. Sweden began investing buffer funds in stocks in 1974. Norway invests part of its oil surplus (which is a general reserve, not earmarked for social security). Switzerland and Canada have moved this way. Some proposals in the US also move this way. In addition to the issue of portfolio choice in DB systems, similar issues arise in DC plans—what are the effects of portfolio diversification? So we can ask what happens if we alter the portfolio of assets held by social security, necessarily adapting benefits or taxes in some way to the changes in realized rates of return over time. The analysis can be considered in three steps. One is what happens within the system. Second is what happens overall to beneficiaries and taxpayers, ignoring general equilibrium feedbacks. And third, what general equilibrium feedbacks might we expect.

To deal with so complicated a subject, I divide the analysis into two parts. First, I will consider a fully funded nonredistributive (at the margin) DC system that has a prespecified portfolio choice and no additional legislation, since this is a fully specified system. Then I will briefly consider DB systems that contain sufficient automatic adjustments that they too are fully specified. That leaves the role of future legislation and of system design in influencing future legislation (relevant for both DB and DC systems), discussed below in the section on political risks. The focus will be on risk allocation, skimming over other aspects of the systems.

Before turning to comparative statics, I want to review the properties of rates of return. I rely on US data. This focus leaves out the large effects that have occurred in some other countries from wars and hyperinflations.[10]

Rates of Return

The rate of return on equities is highly variable. For example, John Cochrane (1997) notes that over the fifty years from 1947 to 1996, the excess return of stocks over Treasury bills was 8.0 percent, but, assuming that annual returns were statistically independent, the

---

[10] For a discussion of returns in the G-5, see Burtless (2001).

standard statistical confidence interval extends from 3.0 to 13 percent. Use of a data set covering a longer period lowers the size of the confidence interval, provided one is willing to assume that the stochastic process describing rates of return is stable for the longer period. But that assumption is somewhat questionable. There are two aspects to this high variability. One is to recognize the market risk taken on by workers as part of a DC system with a diversified portfolio. Second is the fact that replacement rates will vary within and across cohorts. Within cohorts the variation will come from different portfolio choices and from different time shapes of earnings and so of asset purchase. While different portfolios for different workers is part of the point of having a DC system with portfolio choice, the realized outcomes may have unsatisfactory social consequences or induce political responses. Second, since realized histories will vary, even some nearby cohorts will have very different replacement rates. This point has been made very forcibly in the US debate by Burtless (forthcoming). Using historic data, he calculated replacement rates at the time of retirement for workers with smooth earnings who invest fully in stocks and then buy nominal annuities when they retire (assuming the same life expectancy for all cohorts to highlight the role of risky returns). Someone retiring in 1975 would have had a replacement rate that was only 42 percent as large as someone retiring just six years earlier in 1969. Both stock market returns and a change in interest rates contributed to this huge swing in replacement rates. Of course there are strategies to reduce such variation, as we will see in a moment. But that leaves the question of what strategies will actually be adopted.

Alier and Vittas (1999) have examined how much different portfolios can deal with this problem, and I summarize some of their findings. There are three approaches to modeling risk. One is to fit a stochastic model and then simulate. Such a model needs to recognize that the distribution of returns has fat tails compared with a normal distribution and has some mean reversion. Some simulations take that into account. A second approach is simpler, just to run a possible program through historic data. A third approach, bootstrapping, takes historic annual returns, and randomizes their sequence. But, with some predictability in returns as well as mean reversion, this approach is somewhat limited. All of these approaches assume the future will have the same stochastic properties as the past. While a good first assumption, it is not without controversy, with recognition of the likelihood that the risk premium has declined, although there is considerable dispute as to how much it might have declined. The size of a decline would affect one's predictions of the gain from portfolio diversification.[11] And estimates based on the use of the past depend on how much of the past you want to rely on.

Using historic data, Alier and Vittas calculate the range in replacement rates (relative to final earnings) over cohorts, assuming smooth earnings growth. The ratio is large. It can be made smaller by choosing less risky portfolios and by age-varying portfolio strategies, but it remains substantial. Taking on less risk lowers replacement rates on average, but I want to focus on the residual risk and so the range in replacement rates.[12] Paraphrasing their results, they find that if workers save 10 percent of earnings, invest all their funds in equities, earn the historical returns that prevailed in the US equity market between 1871 and 1996, and purchase a real annuity on retirement, the average replacement rate (ARR) across all cohorts equals 61 percent. But they also find that the max/min ratio is slightly over 4, ranging from a maximum of 99.7 percent (for the cohort retiring in 1966) to a minimum of 24.6 percent (1921).

They find that investing everything in bonds results in much lower ARR (22.6 percent), but with little improvement in the max/min ratio (3.78). This is consistent with Siegel's (1998) analysis of the relative risk of stocks and nominal bonds—bonds are riskier than one might have guessed. Indeed using some stocks in an all-nominal-bond portfolio lowers the risk. Investing in a balanced portfolio with 60 percent equities, 30 percent bonds and

[11] For an overview of the future of stock returns, see Diamond (2000). For recent evaluations, see Campbell (2001), Diamond (2001c), and Shoven (2001). For more strongly held views on the decline of the risk premium, see McGratten and Prescott (2001) and Jagannathan *et al.* (2001).

[12] They assume that workers contribute 10% of their wage, their wage grows by the average growth rate (plus 1% to reflect the rising earnings-profile of the average worker), have a total active life of 40 years, and live in retirement for 20 years. They thus abstract from actuarial considerations or from less than full contribution histories. They consider two types of simple annuities: a 2.5% real annuity; and a nominal annuity paying the current nominal yield on 15-year US bonds.

10 percent commercial paper brings the max/min ratio down to 3.15 while lowering the ARR to 42 percent.

Alier and Vittas consider three alternative strategies. The first involves investing everything in equities for the first thirty-five years of work and then implementing a late gradual shift into bonds. The second strategy is to undertake a gradual purchase of annuities, starting five years before retirement. Both of these strategies lower the max/min ratio (to around 3), with a smaller loss in the ARR (now about 53 percent). The third strategy uses a variable annuity, either for all the accumulated capital or for half of it. The results are very impressive. Even with a 50 percent allocation to variable annuities, the max/min ratio falls to 2.42, while the ARR is 72 percent. The replacement rate of the 1921 cohort rises from 25 to 74 percent. It should, however, be stressed that under variable annuities the annual replacement rates themselves vary. The reported cohort replacement rates refer to the average for each cohort over the whole of the retirement life. A max/min ratio of 2.42 still indicates that there are significant problems with replacement rate adequacy for some cohorts. Like others, they view this as part of the case for a multipillar system. Indeed, the trade-off between risk and return suggests that if there are assets, at least some of them should be invested in equities.

Consideration just of consumption in retirement from asset returns leaves out two issues. One is the presence of other decisions before the realization of the rate of return. A prolonged boom followed by a collapse may lead to changes in savings and choices of large investments (e.g. large houses) that have poor consequences. In part this is associated with delays in realization (Dréze and Modigliani, 1987). In part it may be associated with misinterpretation of future prospects based on recent returns, as is plausible for some given both the nature of what appear to be bubbles and responses to surveys showing heavy influence of recent outcomes (Case and Shiller, 1988).

The second question is how people react to the sequence of short-term returns that combine to be the long-term return, particularly those returns that occur shortly before retirement. Insofar as people are accurately described by loss aversion (Kahneman and Tversky, 1979; Tversky and Kahneman, 1992), there is a psychological cost to watching asset values drop shortly before realization and conversion to an annuity. This can have political ramifications as disappointed investors call for bailouts. It also raises significantly the question of social evaluation. Should society ignore such reactions, as is inherent in evaluating outcomes solely in terms of conventional lifetime utility of consumption functions?

I turn now to considering the comparative statics of what happens if a system goes from full investment in government bonds to a diversified portfolio.

Comparative Statics of Portfolio Diversification
In a DC system with a rational representative agent, the portfolio of the social security system would not matter unless the representative agent were put in a corner position that could not be undone. What matters for an agent is the total portfolio, adding assets held within and outside social security. So changing the portfolio of social security would involve an asset swap with the representative agent's non-social security portfolio, a swap which involves no price changes. Thus it is a total wash.

But the representative agent model is not adequate for this problem. Many people hold little or no assets outside social security and these assets may be in the form of housing and precautionary balances, assets that are not readily usable to offset portfolio changes by social security. To consider this situation, together with John Geanakoplos (2001), I have examined what happens in two-agent models, where one agent is the standard agent and the other simply does no saving.[13] We assume that workers without assets do not make a portfolio choice (they do not short one asset to hold another).

The first question is whether the optimal social security portfolio for agents who do no private saving is totally in bonds. While there may be some people who want an all-bond portfolio (Pestieau and Possen, 1999), for most people it makes sense to have at least some stocks. Indeed, as noted above, studies of the historic record in the US of portfolio holdings of stocks and nominal bonds show that having some stocks reduces portfolio variance while increasing expected return, making an all-nominal-bond portfolio

[13] This discussion is based on Diamond and Geanakoplos (2001). For a model of social security portfolio diversification with a fixed cost of investing in stocks and rational decisionmaking, see Abel (2001).

one that is not on the efficient risk-return frontier, based strictly on the historical data (Siegel, 1998). If we were to pursue a detailed evaluation of the implications of an all-bond portfolio choice, we would need to examine the correlation between life-time earnings trajectories and returns on assets, thereby assessing how much correlated risk workers already hold. I will not pursue this line but, based on this brief discussion and the rarity of advice to hold all-bond portfolios, assume that if prices of assets do not change, there is an expected utility gain for the covered labor force from a change to a diversified portfolio. In this discussion, I omit a role for inflation-indexed bonds. While these are very popular with economists, they have had very little public acceptance in the US.

Portfolio diversification by social security involves a trade of assets with rational savers. How does such a portfolio trade affect the rational savers who engage in transactions with social security? If prices do not change, then the willingness of rational savers to engage in transactions shows that they are not made worse off. How might prices not change? Here it is necessary to enter into analysis of the underlying technology that generates the return patterns of financial assets. A sufficient condition for changes in the aggregate portfolios to have no effect on rates of return is that there be linear technologies in investment in safe and risky assets. For example, firms might have an activity ana-lysis technology, showing constant returns to different types of investment. The different types of investment have different risk characteristics (and different expected returns). To keep it simple, assume there are two activities—a risky one and a safe one. Then the technology (assuming that both activities are undertaken in equilibrium) guarantees that prices do not change. In this case, when social security sells bonds and buys stocks, safe investors can accommodate this transaction by increasing investment in the risky technology and decreasing investment in the safe techno-logy. Thus, given the argument that workers are helped by port-folio diversification, in this setting we get a weak Pareto gain. Moreover, overall investment is unchanged but expected output increases since the risky technology must have a higher expected yield (in order to be held in equilibrium by risk-averse investors).

Plausibly, rates of return do change. Plausibly, the rate of return on government bonds goes up and the expected rate of return on risky investment goes down. A change in the rate of return on government bonds requires a change in taxes to finance government debt (at some point in time). My analysis with Geanakoplos focuses on the setting where more of the taxes to finance the debt obligation fall on rational savers than their share of interest received from the government. In this case an increase in the government bond rate and taxes to cover the increased interest cost result in a redistribution from savers to workers, which helps the workers further. In other words, if the portion of the trust fund invested in bonds is earning a higher rate of return after the portfolio change, then workers are better off, provided their taxes do not increase by more than the increase in interest earnings. In addition, redistribution across generations of savers occurs with the presence of long-lived assets, such as land. Their values can go up or down, as we are making risky returns more highly valued by savers (since workers now have part of that) and changing both expected returns and the discount rate of long-lived assets. The change in rates of return and taxes, in turn, can affect investment.

From a welfare perspective, the gain from including workers without savings in the risk sharing is a pure gain. All of the other effects are redistributions. Thus, they would be a wash normatively if the social marginal utility of consumption when old were the same (relative to interest rates) within and across cohorts. Otherwise the evaluation depends on the relative welfare weights of winners and losers.

We can extend this analysis to DB systems by assuming that the government has a rule for adjusting taxes and or benefits as a function of realized returns. The normative value of the portfolio change then depends on how well the government does the adaptation. If done well, which involves responding to estimates of the likely extent of changes in returns—the extent to which they have persistence—the case for stock investments is enhanced. But adjustment can be done badly by government delay in responding to poor market outcomes followed by larger responses with shorter horizons than would occur with a DC system. The tendency to delay inflicting pain makes delay likely, but the political instinct to spread pain widely suggests that the adjustments may not be as sharply concentrated as with a DC system. In addition to the impact on risk, this is likely to involve a different evolution of the degree of funding than would a DC system. This follows if legislation is quicker to raise benefits after positive return surprises than to lower them after negative ones.

This analysis has focused on what will happen in equilibrium from a given portfolio transaction, no other government actions changing except those required by the revenue needs affected by a change in the government interest rate. But it is necessary to ask whether such a portfolio change is likely to be accompanied by other changes. There are two similar effects that are plausible (Smetters, 1997).

Assume that in a DC system with a government selected portfolio, the stock market does very badly after a change in the portfolio. Would the government succeed in leaving the losses on the beneficiaries? It is possible that for losses that are large enough, the government would bail out the retirees so affected, incurring an increase in implicit liability. (Indeed, some US proposals include explicit guarantees.) If this is government behavior, then the change in portfolio includes a guarantee, with the cost of the guarantee shifted to future generations. Indeed, we can consider this to be provision of an option to the holders of the newly diversified portfolio. The government could try to finance this by extra taxes on particularly good earnings (Miles, 2000). But, there are likely to be real asymmetries in the politics of returns on portfolios with retirees keeping good returns and being helped out after bad ones.

A similar effect arises in DB systems. In a DB system, it is common to adapt taxes and benefits to projections of future positions of social security. This would be necessary if there were an attempt to "fully fund" in an actuarial sense. When a system is out of balance, as many are today, some package of reforms may be adopted. If portfolio diversification is part of that package, then it may affect what else is in the package. In particular the effect may be to consider the system in less financial trouble (since the expected return on the portfolio has increased) and so make fewer other cost-saving changes. This is likely to shift expected costs into the future in a similar way to that described above with a guarantee for a DC system. That is, poor returns may imply a payroll tax increase for future workers, while good returns do not imply a tax decrease. Since older generations have a larger share of future benefits than of future taxes, any such asymmetric response works to the benefit of older generations. Even if future reactions to realizations on the portfolio are symmetric, then risk has been shifted forward in time, along with the expected return. If the alternative to portfolio diversification were a less future-oriented adjustment (such as higher taxes now), then the cost of the risk bearing is shifted forward with a portfolio change, putting more burden on the future.

This returns us to the general issue of how portfolio choice for a DB system differs from portfolio choice for a DC system. The difference is in the allocation of the risk from the return on the portfolio. This should be thought of in conjunction with other risks, which are likely to be correlated—low returns in the short run are probably associated with low earnings. Then the question is how the system adapts to variations in this return. Variation may be specified in the law or part of a newly legislated response. One needs a theory of the political determination of the evolving system in response to its financial position in order to answer this question. While a DB system is capable of allocating that risk symmetrically and spread well across cohorts, the political outcome is likely to be asymmetric (involving redistribution across cohorts in an ex ante sense), although the political system is likely to spread both pain and gain widely, which does conform to better risk bearing.

In Sections 3.1 and 3.2, I have looked at risk implications from the perspective of single decisions (annuitization and accumulation). An alternative approach would be to consider the sharing of all the capital risk in an economy. There are four groups available to share that risk—current wealth holders, current workers (some of whom may have little or no financial wealth), current retirees, and future workers and savers. The government can spread some of the capital risk from private wealth holders to the other groups. Such spreading seems sensible. This can involve some use of variable annuities, some use of trust fund portfolio diversification, and some shifting of risk to future benefits and taxes (both inside and outside social security). Since there is a significant correlation over longer periods between capital returns and wage growth rates, similar risk bearing (but not risk sharing) happens with indexing to wages. Also risk sharing happens through the taxation of different tax bases.

3.3. Risk to Cohort-Wide Earnings

In a widely cited article, Merton (1984) identified a role for an unfunded defined benefit social security system in spreading the risk to cohort-wide earnings across cohorts. He described the problem of nontradable human capital risk in contrast with an Arrow–Debreu complete market system. In the Arrow–Debreu setting, workers, at the start, would trade much of the cohort-wide risk to their earnings (ignoring individual insurance issues) and receive in turn some of the risk on capital, of which they hold very little when young. The underlying image is one where all agents share in all risks. At the extreme, a PAYG system relates retirement benefits (in aggregate) to the overall earnings of younger workers, not to their own (earlier) cohort earnings, although there can still be sensitivity to individual earnings. In considering the advantages of such an approach, we can recognize that earnings are far from perfectly correlated with rates of return on assets. Some of cohort-wide earnings risk is already transferred to older contemporary cohorts by the capital market process insofar as earnings affect savings and savings affect asset prices, particularly items like land with relatively inelastic supply and very long life. Merton recognized two ways in which the risk gets transmitted. Insofar as a benefit formula uses wage indexing, high growth of wages of younger workers will raise the wage index and so raise the future retirement benefits of older workers. Moreover, the rate of wage growth affects the financial stability of the US system (given the indexing of benefits just to prices). Therefore the adjustment of benefits to revenue realizations is a second route for spreading this risk.

But a social security system can transfer risks forward in time as well, an aspect of DB systems that Merton does not analyze. Merton focused on risk sharing among those alive at a time, ignoring the ability of a DB system to transfer income across different states into which a cohort might be born (Gale, 1990). In thinking about such risks, a central element is the specification of the intertemporal structure of preferences. Insofar as utility functions in retirement include a factor based on the standards of living to which workers became accustomed earlier in life, then there is less role for risk transmission through a device that works through benefits.

Merton approached the issue of risk sharing by looking for an implicit trade between generations alive at the same time that would be Pareto improving (in a representative agent setting).[14] Recent writings have approached this issue by examining the expected utility of a cohort in a steady-state stochastic equilibrium. Expected utility is related to the mix of PAYG and funded portions of social security. The funded part has an expected return equal to the expected return on assets and the risk characteristics of assets. The unfunded part has an expected rate of return depending on economic growth and the risk characteristics of wage growth (Miles, 2000; Dutta *et al.*, 1999). Thus the analysis contrasts the risky rates of return on assets with the risks associated with cohort-wide earnings. Expected utility can be related to the relative size of the two systems for a given tax rate. The papers conclude that a multi-pillar system, partially DB and partially DC, has good risk characteristics.

We need to be careful about the inferences from this analysis, which is focusing just on the steady state and ignoring the cost of creating the capital for funding. Thus, the finding that replacing some of the DC system by a PAYG DB system helps the steady-state generation carries over to a fuller analysis since decreasing funding can help the transition generation as well. In contrast, replacing part of an unfunded DB system with a funded DC system hurts the transition generation that must provide the funding. Therefore, the gain to the steady-state generations is not necessarily a social welfare gain when considering all generations. Second, reading the conclusion as favoring a two-pillar system ignores the potential in a partially funded DB to also mix capital and labor risks in determining benefits. This alternative does depend on the ability of the government to invest with a DB system, as discussed in Lecture 1. Third, it misses out on the idea that one does not need funding to swap risks. That is, the government has the ability to borrow to invest in other assets, thereby adding capital market risks to an unfunded DB system. More realistically, some taxes on capital income (e.g. the estate tax) could be earmarked for part of social security as a swap with part

---

[14] He also considered using consumption taxes to finance services for the young as part of this implicit trade, since the elderly are a larger share of consumption than of income.

of payroll tax revenue. That is, the government has the ability, through the tax and transfer mechanism to swap capital market risks for wage level risks among different groups. Thus, there are multiple approaches to getting desirable risk characteristics.

However, there is a related issue of how large a mandated savings system should be. If it makes sense to leave considerable room for voluntary private retirement savings, then that savings will be funded, providing the same kind of diversified system.[15]

3.4. Risks in the Political Process[16]

It is common to hear the statement that DC systems expose workers to market risk, but DB systems expose them to political risk. This contrast is wrong on two counts. One is that DC systems are not without political risks. Second, DB systems are not without market risks.[17] I want to discuss political risks in both types of ongoing systems. I will not discuss in detail the political risks in initial legislation creating a system or fundamentally changing a system, although these are important. For example, in the US, there are proposals that remove all redistribution from social security, except that coming through uniform annuitization. Such proposals are taken seriously when they are part of an individual account plan, even though they do not include any change in protecting the poor outside the system. Such proposals would not be taken seriously if they were merely to switch the progressive social security benefit formula to be linear. Thus, a distributional outcome that is politically settled (not under serious discussion) can become politically unsettled when the basic institutional structure is on the table. This is a source of risk, whether one anticipates a better or worse overall distribution after the debate (Heclo, 1998).

I find it useful to think about political risk in three pieces. The first is useful legislative responses to changing economic and demographic circumstances. Second is costly legislative responses

---

[15] For a discussion of how big the savings mandate should be, see Diamond (1995).

[16] For an earlier pass at these issues, see Diamond (1996).

[17] Market risks are present if the DB system has assets. Moreover, high inflation is also a market risk in both systems, although I do not discuss it. And economic crises can threaten both kinds of systems, as we have seen recently in Argentina.

to changing circumstances. And third is legislative response to changing political constellations.

Market and contractual incompleteness is the starting place for my discussion. In the Arrow–Debreu model, everyone starts out with a complete list of the states of nature and the opportunity to trade conditional on each of them, and then, all of this trade is coordinated perfectly once and for all. This perspective (while it has been exceptionally helpful for organizing economic thought) goes wrong on the first step. No one has a complete list of the states of nature. So, whatever one plans now, it will be worthwhile to adapt the plans in the future. This perspective is also key to making good sense of the rules versus discretion debate in macroeconomics. Rules look great if you really do know the model of the economy. But we do not "really" know it in that sense, and the role of discretion is to adapt to what was misunderstood, or what changes. After all economic institutions do not show the behavioral stability of electrons.

Legislation does not attempt to have taxes and benefits that adapt fully, according to prespecified rules, to all changing economic and demographic circumstance. Rather, indexation is included to some circumstances, and others are left outside the formal rules. Here we come to the first difference between DB and DC systems. When the world changes, a DB system is likely to have financial consequences that either require more resources or permit the use of fewer resources. It may also happen that the overall financial balance is not altered, but a DB system functions less well anyway. Changing family patterns can make benefit rules no longer as good as what was anticipated. Or changing life expectancies or income distribution can make the distributional pattern less satisfactory. In contrast, a DC system adapts financially (assuming the survival of the institutions absorbing risk, such as the insurers providing annuities). But a DC system can function less satisfactorily for the same reasons that change the financial position of a DB system.

As an example of useful legislative responses, consider what might happen if people start living much longer after retirement. A DB system has financial problems, to which a legislature can respond by a combination of increased taxes and decreased benefits. Legislatures can vary in how well they do this adaptation— how long the lead time, how widely the changes are spread, how much they are concentrated in places where the risk is borne more cheaply. A DC system adapts by having lower benefits, which may now be inadequate benefits for part of the population. A legislature can adapt by changing mandated contributions and by having transfers inside or outside the social security system. Successfully done, such legislation improves the risk-bearing quality of either system. But we can ask how well we expect this to be done. A DB system has a tendency to be asymmetric— sharing gains with current generations and shifting losses to future ones. A DB system is subject to delays in legislation that magnify the size of the changes per person when they do happen, although projected financial needs of a DB system create some pressure to legislate change prior to a full-blown crisis.

There is no analogous force for an increase in a mandated savings rate in a DC system, although some weak force may come eventually, if there is an increase in the poverty rate of the elderly, along with an increase in the cost of general revenue financed anti-poverty programs. Thus a DC system is also subject to nonresponses—nonresponses that can leave the system working considerably less well. The absence of a financial crisis for the system does not imply that it is working well. A DC system also has an asymmetry from not being totally immune to financial rescues after particularly bad outcome even though particularly good returns are much less likely to be tapped for other government purposes. It is good that rescues sometimes happen, but maybe they happen too often (given their effect on incentives).[18] Maybe. I am reminded of David Warsh's observation that from a moral hazard point of view the real tragedy of the Titanic was the people rescued, not those who drowned. Modeling of political behavior, for which formal models have not gotten very far, is needed for thorough characterization of the stochastic properties of the different systems. Static median voter models, while a useful first step, do not come too close to describing how representative democracies work.

---

[18] The real issue is not moreover fewer rescues in total, but more of some kind and fewer of others. This is similar to my attitude toward the level of government spending. Analysts generally want more spending on some projects and less on others. Of course, analysts disagree about which projects should get more and which less.

For a retirement income system to work well, it needs to be reasonably reliable. So significant responses of the retirement system to temporary economic phenomena are an example of costly legislative responses. The central variable that we worry about in this context is the state of the rest of the government budget. If the government is currently short of cash, it will be tempted to tap the social security system for it. For a DB system to have annual adjustments of benefit levels to deal with other budgetary problems is a sign of political failure. And we see a lot of that. Germany, currently, is a striking example. This is more likely with a DB system where the benefits flow through the government. But there is a similar problem for DC systems—the government can pay below-market interest rates on government debt that it requires social security to hold. While these do not show up in benefits as quickly, they are still a problem. In which of these settings is this problem more likely to cause difficulty? That depends on the quality of government. Some governments will tap anything in sight that they can lay their hands on, and the stock of assets in mandated savings accounts may be particularly easy to tap. With better governments, the DC system may be better insulated from this type of political risk. That has been the case in Chile. Some governments could keep either system on a pretty even keel. A similar long-run issue arises on the connection between funding social security and using the funding as a vehicle to increase national savings. If funding just leads to larger deficits on the rest of the budget, then national savings are not increased. And adequate national savings can happen without funding social security. Both patterns can arise in either system.

Also, an issue is the redistribution that happens within social security. This may reflect political power rather than more general normative considerations. One way in which this has happened in some countries is through the presence of multiple DB systems with different rules. Then there can be redistribution across systems. For example, in Chile there were separate DB systems for white- and blue-collar workers. The one for white-collar workers was more generous. Having a single unitary system for the entire covered population seems to help with politics. (This is not meant to say that civil servants should not also have a secondary system, as do employees of large corporations.) So, in one political setting DB systems may have worse distributional outcomes than would a DC system, while in other political settings the reverse can be true.

I turn next to purely political phenomena (as opposed to political reactions to economic events). The desired pattern of distribution, either across or within generations can change. In part, a current legislature should not (cannot) bind the hands of all future legislatures on this issue. It is appropriate for changes in fundamental views to lead to changes in institutions. But sometimes what happens is a see-saw as political forces alternate and social security might become a political football. Again, this can happen in either system. But it will happen differently in the two systems. Part of this is the playing out of distributional elements differently in different systems, as discussed in the first lecture. That is, redistribution built into a social security system may be less likely to have a political see-saw than stand-alone redistribution rules. Another example comes with annuitization. DB systems are naturally organized with annuitized benefits, although there could be lump-sum options. A DC system needs to have an explicit process for converting accumulations into annuities. This can raise the question of whether mandatory annuitization is a sustainable political outcome. Insofar as lump sum withdrawals (not the type of phased withdrawal present in Chile) lead to more rapid spending, they may hurt the long-lived beneficiaries, who may predominantly be widows in a system with significant benefits for surviving spouses.

While, in principle, a DB system can accomplish lots of good things, the appropriate question to ask is how well we would expect a system to do these. For example, the NDC system avoids some of these risk-sharing devices in order to hew more closely to the image of a DC system. So it is a type of DB system that is striking a particular balance between heading off the need for some interventions that might be poorly done at a cost of making less likely other interventions that might be good. For example, by having automatic adjustment of benefits to fully offset the financial implications of increased life expectancy, an NDC system is likely to adapt more slowly to a need for more resources to finance longer retirements than is a standard DB system. On the other hand, by basing benefits on taxes paid, not earnings subject to tax, an NDC system is likely to be more generous to the future than would a standard DB system when taxes are anticipated or legislated to increase. Both systems can be manipulated to help special groups. A standard DB can have different benefit formulae and different retirement ages for different industries. It can also have different tax rates, for example, between employed and self-employed (as was the case in the past in the US). But since this shows up in immediate revenues, it may be less likely to occur and endure than the similar pattern under an NDC system of crediting some workers with higher tax rates than they actually pay. This type of response to political power is an issue in Italy.

3.5. Concluding Remarks

Because of its size and its connection with work, retirement, and national savings, social security is extremely important for economic outcomes generally and the workings of the labor and capital markets in particular. The complexity of patterns in both market and government arrangements makes for many links between social security and economic equilibrium. Studying these links is fascinating. Sometimes it may also help in the quest for better economic policy.

References

AARON, HENRY (1966), 'The social insurance paradox', *Canadian Journal of Economics and Political Science*, 32(3): 371–7.

ABEL, ANDREW (2001), 'The effects of investing social security funds in the stock market when fixed costs prevent some households from holding stocks', *American Economic Review*, 91(1): 128–48.

ALIER, MAX, and DIMITRI VITTAS (1999), 'Personal pension plans and stock market volatility', Development Research Group, World Bank (Unpublished).

ARNOLD, R. DOUGLAS (1990), *The Logic of Congressional Action*. (New Haven: Yale University Press).

BAYER, PATRICK, B. DOUGLAS BERNHEIM, and JOHN KARL SCHOLZ (1996), 'The effects of financial education in the workplace: Evidence from a survey of employers.' Working Paper 5655, NBER.

BERNHEIM, B. DOUGLAS, JONATHAN SKINNER, and STEVEN WEINBERG (2001), 'What accounts for the variation in retirement wealth among U.S. households?' *American Economic Review*, 91(4): 832–57.

BODIE, ZVI, and DWIGHT CRANE (1997), 'Personal investing: Advice, theory, and evidence', *Financial Analysts' Journal*, 57(6): 13–23.

BOHN, HENNING (2001), 'Social security and demographic uncertainty: The risk-sharing properties of alternative policies', in *Risk Aspects of Investment-Based Social Security Reform*, ed. J. Campbell and M. Feldstein (Chicago: University of Chicago Press) pp. 203–46.

BOSKIN, MICHAEL, LAURENCE KOTLIKOFF, and JOHN SHOVEN (1988), *A Proposal for Fundamental Social Security Reform in the 21st Century*. (Lexington: Lexington Books).

BREYER, FRIEDRICH (1989), 'On the intergenerational Pareto efficiency of pay-as-you-go financed pension systems', *Journal of International and Theoretical Economics*, 145: 643–58.

BROWN, JEFFREY (2001), 'How should we insure longevity risk in pensions and social security?' Issue in Brief, Center for Retirement Research, Boston College.

BRUGIAVINI, AGAR (1993), 'Uncertainty resolution and the timing of annuity purchases', *Journal of Political Economy*, 50(1): 31–62.

BURKHAUSER, RICHARD, KENNETH COUCH, and JOHN PHILLIPS (1996), 'Who takes early social security benefits? The economic and health characteristics of early beneficiaries', *The Gerontologist*, 36(6): 789–99.

—— and TIMOTHY SMEEEDING (1994), 'Social security reform: A budget neutral approach to reducing older women's disproportionate risk of poverty'. Policy Brief, Maxwell School, Syracuse University.

BURTLESS, GARY (2001), 'Asset accumulation and retirement income under individual retirement accounts: Evidence from five countries.' Brookings. Paper prepared for the Third International Forum of the Collaboration Projects on Aging Issues, Economic and Social Research Institute, September 17–19, 2001, Tokyo, Japan (unpublished).

—— (forthcoming), 'Social security privatization and financial market risk: Lessons from U.S. financial history', in *Social Security Reform in Advanced Countries*, ed. T. Ihori and T. Tachibanaki (London and New York: Routledge).

CAMPBELL, JOHN (2001), 'Forecasting US stock returns in the 21st century', in *Estimating the Real Rate of Return on Stocks Over the Long Term*, Social Security Advisory Board, pp. 3–10 (web address http://www.ssab. gov/estimated%20rate%20of%20return.pdf) (unpublished).

CASE, KARL, and ROBERT SHILLER (1988), 'The behavior of home buyers in boom and post-boom markets', *New England Economic Review*, November/December, 29–46.

COCHRANE, JOHN (1997), 'Where is the market going? Uncertain facts and novel theories', *Federal Reserve Bank of Chicago Economic Perspectives*, 21(6): 3–37.

COILE, COURTNEY, PETER DIAMOND, JONATHAN GRUBER, and ALAIN JOUSTEN (1999), 'Delays in claiming social security benefits', Working Paper 7318, NBER.

Consultant Panel on Social Security Reform (1976), *Report to the Congressional Research Service* (Washington: US Government Printing Office).

COSTA, DORA (1998), *The Evolution of Retirement: An American Economic History 1880–1990* (Chicago: University of Chicago Press for NBER).

—— (2000), 'American living standards, 1888–1994: Evidence from consumer expenditures', Working Paper 7650, NBER.

CRAWFORD, VINCENT, and DAVID LILIEN (1981), 'Social security and the retirement decision', *Quarterly Journal of Economics*, 96(3): 505–29.

DAHLQUIST, MAGNUS, STEFAN ENGSTROM, and PAUL SODERLIND (1999), 'Performance and characteristics of Swedish mutual funds 1993–97', Stockholm School of Economics.

DALBAR, Inc. (1993), *1993 Quantitative Analysis of Investor Behavior*.

DAVIDOFF, THOMAS, JEFFREY BROWN, and PETER DIAMOND (2001), 'Annuities and individual welfare', MIT, Unpublished.

DIAMOND, PETER (1994), 'Pension reform in a transition economy: Notes on Poland and Chile', in *The Transition in Eastern Europe*, ed. O. Blanchard, K. Froot, and J. Sachs (Chicago: University of Chicago Press) pp. 71–83.

—— (1995), 'Government provision and regulation of economic support in old age', in *Annual Bank Conference on Development Economics*, ed. M. Bruno and B. Plesovic (Washington, DC: The World Bank) pp. 83–103.

—— (1996), 'Insulation of pensions from political risk', in *The Economics of Pensions: Principles, Policies and International Experience*, ed. S. Valdés-Prieto (Cambridge: Cambridge University Press) pp. 33–57.

—— (1997), 'Macroeconomic aspects of social security reform', *Brookings Papers on Economic Activity*, 2: 1–87.

—— (1998), 'Optimal income taxation: An example with a U-shaped pattern of optimal marginal tax rates', *American Economic Review*, 88(1): 83–95.

—— (1999*a*), 'Issues in privatizing social security, report of an expert panel of the national academy of social insurance.' (Cambridge: MIT Press). Edited volume.

—— (1999*b*), 'Social security reform with a focus on Italy', *Revista Di Politica Economica*, 89(12): 11–27.

—— (2000*a*), 'Administrative costs and equilibrium charges with individual accounts', in *Administrative Costs and Social Security Privatization*, ed. J. Shoven (Chicago: University of Chicago Press) pp. 137–72.

—— (2000*b*), 'Social security reform with a focus on Sweden', *Ekonomisk Debatt*, 28(3): 229–41.

—— (2000*c*), 'What stock market returns to expect for the future', *Social Security Bulletin*, 63(2) 38–52.

—— (2001*a*), 'Social security reform with a focus on the Netherlands', *De Economist*, 149(1): 1–12.

—— (2001*b*), 'Issues in social security reform with a focus on Spain.' Unpublished, MIT.

—— (2001*c*), 'What stock market returns to expect for the future: An update.' In *Estimating the Real Rate of Return on Stocks Over the Long Term*, Social Security Advisory Board, pp. 11–16 (web address http://www.ssab.gov/estimated%20rate%20of%20return.pdf) (unpublished).

—— (forthcoming), *Taxation, Incomplete Markets and Social Security*, The 2000 Munich Lectures (Cambridge: MIT Press).

—— and JOHN GEANAKOPLOS (2001), 'Social security investment in equities I: Linear case', Cowles Foundation Discussion Paper.

—— and JONATHAN GRUBER (1999), 'Social security and retirement in the U.S.', in *Social Security and Retirement Around the World*, ed. J. Gruber and D. Wise (Chicago) pp. 437–73.

—— and BOTOND KOSZEGI (1999), 'Quasi-hyperbolic discounting and retirement.' Working Paper, MIT.

—— and JAMES MIRRLEES (1978), 'A model of social insurance with variable retirement', *Journal of Public Economics*, 10(3): 295–336.

DIAMOND, PETER and JAMES MIRRLEES (1986), 'Payroll-tax financed social insurance with variable retirement', *Scandinavian Journal of Economics*, 88(1): 25–50.

—— (2000) 'Adjusting one's standard of living: Two period models', in *Incentives, Organization and Public Economics, Papers in Honour of Sir James Mirrlees*, ed. P. J. Hammond and G. D. Myles (Oxford: Oxford University Press) pp. 107–22.

—— (forthcoming), 'Social insurance with variable retirement and private saving.' *Journal of Public Economics*..

—— and MICHAEL ROTHSCHILD (1989), *Uncertainty in Economics (Revised Edition)*, (New York: Academic Press).

—— and SALVADOR VALDÉS-PRIETO (1993), 'Social security reform', in *The Chilean Economy: Policy Lessons and Challenges*, ed. B. Bosworth, R. Dornbusch, and R. Laban (Washington: Brookings Institution) pp. 257–320.

DRÈZE, JACQUES, and FRANCO MODIGLIANI (1987), 'Earnings, assets and savings: A model of interdependent choice', in *Essays on economic decisions under uncertainty*, ed. J. Drèze pp. 213–19.

DULITZKY, DANIEL (1998), 'Social security reforms, retirement plans, and saving under labor income uncertainty', MIT Ph.D. Dissertation.

DUTTA, JAYASRI, SANDEEP KAPUR, and J. MICHAEL ORSZAG (1999), 'A Portfolio Approach to the Optimal Funding of Pensions', Birkbeck College, London, (unpublished).

ELMENDORF, DOUGLAS, and JEFFREY LIEBMAN (2000), 'Social security reform and national saving in an era of budget surpluses', *Brookings Papers on Economic Activity*, 2: 1–52.

FELDSTEIN, MARTIN (1974), 'Social security, induced retirement, and aggregate capital accumulation', *The Journal of Political Economy*, 82(5): 905–26.

GALE, DOUGLAS (1990), 'The efficient design of public debt', in *Public Debt Management: Theory and History*, ed. R. Dornbusch and M. Draghi (Cambridge: Cambridge University Press) pp. 14–47.

GEANAKOPLOS, JOHN, OLIVIA S. MITCHELL, and STEPHEN P. ZELDES (1998), 'Would a privatized social security system really pay a higher rate of return?' in *Framing the Social Security Debate, Values, Politics and Economics*, ed. R. D. Arnold, M. Graetz, and A. Munnell (Washington: National Academy of Social Insurance, distributed by Brookings Institution Press) pp. 137–56.

GILLION, COLION, JOHN TURNER, CLIVE BAILEY, and DENIS LATULIPPE, (eds) (2000) *Social Security Pensions*. (London: International Labour Office). pp. 320–4.

GRUBER, JONATHAN, and DAVID WISE (1999), 'Introduction and Summary', in *Social Security and Retirement Around the World*, ed. J. Gruber and D. Wise (Chicago: University of Chicago Press) pp. 1–35.

—— and PETER ORSZAG (2000), 'Does the social security earnings test affect labor supply and benefits receipt?' Working Paper 2000-07, Boston College.

HASSLER, JOHN, and ASSAR LINDBECK (1997), 'Intergenerational risk sharing, stability and optimality of alternative pension systems.' Research Discussion Paper 1774, CEPR.

HECLO, HUGH (1998), 'A Political Science Perspective on Social Security Reform', in *Framing the Social Security Debate, Values, Politics and Economics*, ed. R. D. Arnold, M. Graetz and A. Munnell (Washington: National Academy of Social Insurance, distributed by Brookings Institution Press) pp. 65–89.

HOLDEN, KAREN, and CATHLEEN ZICK (1998), 'Insuring against the consequences of widowhood in a reformed social security system', in *Framing the Social Security Debate, Values, Politics and Economics*, ed. R. D. Arnold, M. Graetz, and A. Munnell (Washington: National Academy of Social Insurance, distributed by Brookings Institution Press) pp. 157–70.

HOMBURG, STEFAN (2000), 'Ein schnellkurs in sachen rentenreform', *Perspektiven der Wirtschaftspolitik*, 1: 379–82.

HURD, MICHAEL D., DANIEL MCFADDEN, and ANGELA MERRILL (1999), 'Predictors of mortality among the elderly.' Working Paper 7440, NBER.

JAGANNATHAN, RAVI, ELLEN MCGRATTAN, and ANNA SCHERBINA (2001), 'The declining US equity premium', *Federal Reserve Bank of Minnesota Quarterly*, 24(4): 3–19.

KAHN, JAMES (1988), 'Social security, liquidity, and early retirement', *Journal of Public Economics*, 35(1): 97–118.

KAHNEMAN, DANIEL, and AMOS TVERSKY (1979), 'Prospect theory: An analysis of decisions under risk', *Econometrica*, 47(2): 313–27.

—— PAUL SLOVIC, and AMOS TVERSKY (1982), *Judgment Under Uncertainty: Heuristics and Biases.* (Cambridge: Cambridge University Press).

KINGSON, ERIC R, and YVONNE ARSENAULT (2000), 'The diversity of risk among age-62 retired worker beneficiaries.' Working paper CRR WP 2000-08, Center for Retirement Research at Boston College.

LAIBSON, DAVID (1997), 'Golden eggs and hyperbolic discounting', *Quarterly Journal of Economic*, 112(2): 443–78.

—— ANDREA REPETTO, and JEREMY TOBACMAN (1998), 'Self-control and saving for retirement', *Brookings Papers on Economic Activity*, 1: 91–196.

LEONESIO, MICHAEL, DENTON VAUGHAN, and BERNARD WIXON (2000), 'Early retirees under social security: Health status and economic resources.' Working paper 86, Social Security Administration, Office of Policy, Office of Research, Evaluation and Statistics.

LINDAHL, ERIK (1958 (1919)), *Die Gerechtigkeit der Besteurung. Lund: Gleerup. Partial Translation as "Just Taxation—a Positive Solution"* (London: Macmillan).

MCGRATTAN, ELLEN, and EDWARD PRESCOTT (2001), 'Is the stock market overvalued?' *Federal Reserve Bank of Minnesota Quarterly*, 24(4): 20–40.

MERTON, ROBERT (1984), 'On the role of social security as a means for efficient risk-bearing in an economy where human capital is not tradeable', in *Financial Aspects of the U.S. Pension System*, ed. Z. Bodie and J. Shoven (Chicago: University of Chicago Press) pp. 325–58.

MILES, DAVID (2000), 'Funded and unfunded pension schemes: Risk return and welfare.' Working Paper 239, CESifo.

MITCHELL, OLIVIA, JAMES POTERBA, JEFFREY BROWN, and MARK WARSHAWSKY (1999), 'New evidence of the money's worth of individual annuities', *The American Economic Review*, 89(5): 1299–318.

MODIGLIANI, FRANCO, and MARIA LUISA CEPRINI (1998), 'Social security reform: A proposal for Italy', *Review of Economic Conditions in Italy*, 2: 177–201.

——,—— and ARUN S. MURALIDHAR (2000), 'A solution to the social security crisis from an MIT team.' Sloan Working Paper 4051 (Fourth Revision).

MUNNELL, ALICIA (1974), 'The impact of social security on personal savings', *National Tax Journal*, 27(4): 553–67.

—— and ANNIKA SUNDÉN (1999), 'Investment practices of state and local pension plans', in *The Next Challenge: Pensions in the Public Sector*, ed. O. Mitchell and E. Hustead (The Pension Research Council and University of Pennsylvania Press) pp. 153–94.

MURPHY, KEVIN, and FINIS WELCH (1998), 'Perspectives on the social security crisis and proposed solutions', *American Economic Review*, 88(2): 142–50.

MURTHI, MAMTA, J. MICHAEL ORSZAG, and PETER ORSZAG (forthcoming), 'Administrative costs under a decentralized approach to individual accounts: Lessons from the UK experience', in *New Ideas About Old-Age Security: Towards Sustainable Pension Systems in the 21st Century*, ed. R. Holzmann and J. Stiglitz (World Bank/OUP).

MUSGRAVE, RICHARD (1959), *The theory of public finance.* (New York: McGraw Hill).

ODEAN, TERRANCE, and BRAD M. BARBER (2000), 'Trading is hazardous to your wealth: The common stock investment performance of individual investors', *The Journal of Finance*, 55(2): 773–806.

O'DONOGHUE, TED, and MATTHEW RABIN (1999), 'Procrastination in preparing for retirement', in *Behavioral dimensions of retirement economics*, ed. H. Aaron (Washington: Brookings Institution Press and Russell Sage Foundation) pp. 125–56.

Panel on Social Security Financing (1975), *Report to the Committee on Finance, US Senate*, (Washington: US Government Printing Office).

PESTIEAU, PIERRE, and URI POSSEN (1999), 'Investing social security in the equity market. Does it make a difference?' University of Liège (unpublished).

QUINN, JOSEPH (1997), 'The role of bridge jobs in the retirement patterns of older Americans in the 1990s', in *Retirement Prospects in a Defined Contribution World*, ed. D. Salisbury (Washington: Employee Benefit Research Institute) pp. 25–39.

REA, JOHN D, BRIAN K. REID, and TRAVIS LEE (1999), 'Mutual fund costs, 1980–1998.' *Investment Company Institute Perspective*.

ROFMAN, RAFAEL (2000), 'The pension system in Argentina six years after the reform.' Unpublished, World Bank.

SCHMIDT-HEBBEL, KLAUS (1999), 'Latin America's pension revolution: A review of approaches and experience.' Unpublished, Central Bank of Chile.

SHAFIR, ELDAR, PETER DIAMOND, and AMOS TVERSKY (1997), 'Money illusion.' *Quarterly Journal of Economics*, 112(2): 341–74.

SHESHINSKI, EYTAN (1999), 'Annuities and retirement.' Department of Economics, The Hebrew University of Jerusalem.

SHILLER, ROBERT (1993), *Macro Markets: Creating Institutions for Managing Society's Largest Economic Risks, Clarendon Lectures*, (Oxford: Oxford University Press).

SHOVEN, JOHN (2001), 'What are reasonable long-run rates of return to expect on equities?' In *Estimating the Real Rate of Return on Stocks Over the Long Term*, Unpublished, Social Security Advisory Board, pp. 47–53 (web address http://www.ssab.gov/estimated%20rate%20of%20return.pdf).

SIEGEL, JEREMY (1998), *Stocks for the Long Run, 2nd ed.* (New York: McGraw-Hill).

SINN, HANS-WERNER (1999), 'Pension reform and demographic crisis: Why a funded system is needed and why it is not needed.' Working Paper 195 CESifo.

SMETTERS, KENT (1997), 'Investing the social security trust fund in equity: An options pricing approach.' Technical Paper 1997–1, Congressional Budget Office, Macroeconomic Analysis and Tax Analysis Divisions.

TVERSKY, AMOS, and DANIEL KAHNEMAN (1992), 'Advances in prospect theory: Cumulative representation of uncertainty', *Journal of Risk and Uncertainty*, 5(4): 297–323.

VALDÉS-PRIETO, SALVADOR (1997), 'The economics of pensions: Introduction and overview.' In *'The Economics of Pensions: Principles, Policies and International Experience'* (Cambridge: Cambridge University Press) pp. 1–30.

VALDÉS-PRIETO, SALVADOR (1998), 'Risks in pensions and annuities: efficient design.' Social Protection Group, The World Bank.

von WEIZSAECKER, JAKOB (2000), 'Hayek's obvious corollary.' Unpublished, University of Munich.

WICKSELL, KNUT (1958 (1896)), 'A new principle of just taxation.' In *Classics in the theory of Public Finance*, ed. R. Musgrave and A. Peacock (London: Macmillan) pp. 72–118.

World Bank (1994), *Averting the Old Age Crisis: Policies to Protect the Old and Promote Growth. A Policy Research Report* (New York: Oxford University Press).

YAARI, MENACHEM (1965), 'Uncertain lifetime, life insurance, and the theory of the consumer', *Review of Economic Studies*, 32(2): 137–50.

Index